W9-CTC-435

Children's Crafts

By the Editors of Sunset Books
and Sunset Magazine

Lane Publishing Co. • Menlo Park, California

Acknowledgments...

Many boys and girls helped in the preparation of this book. Our very special thanks go to Carol Arguero, Liz Arms, Kenny Bavoris, Laura Bennett, Jeanette Benson, Susanna Block, Danny Boles, Eileen Bordy, Ken Braasch, Stacey Buhler, Marianne Chowning, Alexandra and Rebecca Dahl, Angela DiVecchio, Tasauna Euwing, Craig Farnham, Brenda, Sean, and Sharon Flanagan, Brian Garr, Matthew Gonzalez, Heather and Jessica Graef, Lisa Grinstead, Samantha and Will Hartley, Adrienne Hayes, Jason Heine, Jennifer Henseley, Chris and Trig Isaacson, Lena Jang, Leah and Miriam Kirkman, Laura Klainer, Britt London, Sabra Loney, Mike Maciay, William Marsh, David and Donald Martinson, David McKinnon, John and Paul McManus, Dana Mortenson, Colleen Mullins, Stacey Nash, Matthew Neagle, Steven Nilli, Emily Oliver, Jeff Podlone, Randy Popp, Jennifer Pratt, Matthew and Michelle Prentiss, Christina Ruotolo, Brian Schmidt, Julie Schmidt, Bobby Schunk, Micah Silver, Stephanie Smith, Shelly Stevenson, Chase Stigall, Mandy Veith, Chris Wallace, Gwynneth and Natasha Warton, Allison and Erik Welke, and Karen Wilson.

For liberally sharing their ideas and time, we're also very grateful to Kay Alexander, Marie Anido, Ruth Asawa's Alvarado Art Project at Yerba Buena School, Bonnie Baskin, Junior Arts Center (City of Los Angeles Municipal Art Department), Lynn Masaoka, M. H. de Young Museum Art School, Pat Mullins, Virginia Van Nuys, and Anne Wallace.

We are particularly grateful to Darrow M. Watt for his warm and appealing photographs of children and to Lynne B. Morrall for her valuable ideas and assistance with the photography.

Research and Text: Susan Warton

Supervising Editor: Barbara J. Braasch

Design: JoAnn Masaoka

Illustrations: Dennis Ziemienski

Cover: Fold-up puppet (see page 21).
 Photographed by Darrow M. Watt.
Title Page: Cotton Sock Dolls (see page 39).
 Photographed by Darrow M. Watt.

Executive Editor, Sunset Books: David E. Clark

First Printing April 1976
Copyright © 1976, Lane Publishing Co., Menlo Park, CA 94025. Second Edition. World rights reserved. No part of this publication may be reproduced by any mechanical, photographic, or electronic process or in the form of a phonographic recording, nor may it be stored in a retrieval system, transmitted, or otherwise copied for public or private use without prior written permission from the publisher. Library of Congress No. 75-26496. SBN Title No. 376-04122-6. Lithographed in the United States.

Paper sculpture masks, page 23

Contents

Paper Play

The craft possibilities of paper are just about endless. You'll find a wide variety of craft paper available. Dime stores sell colorful tissue, crepe, and construction paper—as well as bright, glossy shelf paper. Newspaper plants sometimes sell large end rolls of newsprint for low prices. For special projects and beautiful results, it's worth trying good paper from an art supply store: fine drawing paper, rice paper, and different weights of colored cardboard.

Sometimes the most exciting thing to do with paper is to draw or paint on it. But there are many other possibilities with paper—folding a puppet, curling a bird, pleating a fan, cutting out lace, or molding a hat. You'll come up with more ideas as you try some of the following projects.

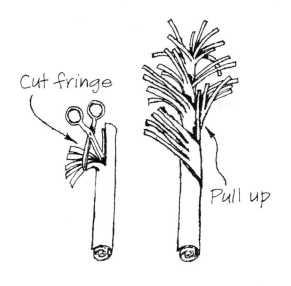

Cut fringe

Pull up

Tall Trees

Would you believe that one newspaper could make a whole forest of trees?

To make a tree, roll up the long side of one newspaper sheet and tape it closed. Cut one end of the roll into a fringe (long snips, fairly close together). Reach inside the fringed end of the roll and carefully pull out the center. This will make the tree spiral up until it's tall. The fringes become leaves that you can curl, pleat, or dress up with paper flowers.

Stand the trees in clay bases or set them in toilet paper rolls taped to a cardboard base.

Foil Folks

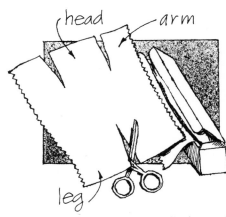

head   arm

leg

Even though aluminum foil doesn't come from trees as paper does, it acts much like paper.

To make a folk, cut a large square of foil in three places, following the sketch above. Wrinkle the top left and right parts into arms. Mold a head out of the middle. Form legs from the two bottom halves. Keep molding until your folk is doing something—maybe playing tennis or dancing.

Stretchy Paper

By cutting slits in a pleated sheet of paper, you can make the paper stretch. Follow the pattern on the right. Use typing paper, shelf paper, wallpaper, or some other kind of strong paper that will stretch without tearing.

One use for stretchy paper is to pretend it's an accordion. Roll it into a cylinder and tape it closed. Poke your fingers through the slits at each end. Sing a catchy tune.

Cut slits

Roll and tape to make accordion.

When the sun shines, this mobile glows. It's made of crayon chips melted between sheets of wax paper. The wire sculpture frames are coat hangers. Directions are given on the opposite page.

Glowing crayon-resist pictures are drawn with fluorescent colors. Directions appear on the opposite page.

Crayon rubbings make nice gift wraps. These designs come from plastic spectacles, a woven place mat, and a fancy iron trivet. Read about crayon rubbings on the opposite page.

Watery colors from melted crayons make delightful prints. They're good for Christmas or birthday cards— or just for a plain old cheerful greeting. See the opposite page for directions.

Black Magic Pictures

The secret of these paintings is fluorescent crayons. Their colors glow brightly through a wash of black paint.

Press hard as you draw —fill in with plenty of thick coloring. Then brush your picture with black poster paint, diluted with water until it's quite thin. Brush with long, sweeping strokes. The wax crayon "resists" the paint, so your drawing will show through against a black background.

Rubbings

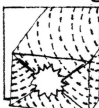

Rubbing is much like tracing except that your finished design is more shaded. It has a slightly three-dimensional look.

Use shelf paper, rice paper, or onionskin typing paper. Lay the paper over whatever you decide to rub. Tape the edges down and rub with the flat side of a crayon, bright chalk, or a pencil.

Here are a few things that take rubbings well: coins, leaves, doilies, fancy iron railings, tiles, engraved metal signs, and bricks.

Crayon Melt Prints

To make these glorious prints, you need a food warming tray that is covered with aluminum foil. When the tray is warm, make a crayon design on the foil. The crayon melts as you draw, producing beautiful trails of color.

To make the print, lay paper over the crayon design. Put on oven mitts and carefully smooth the paper down. Lift it off and see what happened. Wipe the foil with a rag and start a new print.

Sunshine Mobile

Put this together like a sandwich—but do it on the ironing board (protected by an old cloth). First, lay down a big sheet of waxed paper. For the filling, sprinkle the paper with tiny chips of crayons—the more, the better. You might also add colored string and shreds of tissue paper. When it looks good, lay another piece of wax paper over it. Cover the sandwich with a cloth; then press it with a warm iron until the crayon chips are melted.

Bend a thin coat hanger into an interesting shape and glue the sandwich to it. Hang one or several in a sunny window.

Draw on foil-covered warming tray.

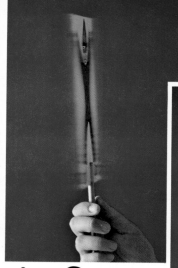

Jumping George

Draw George with flow pens on a recipe card. On one side he stands still, arms at his side. On the flip side, he jumps. Tape the card to an unsharpened pencil. It stays on longer if you cut a slot in the pencil first. To set George in motion, revolve the pencil back and forth between your palms.

Rainbow Fan

Make a striped rainbow fan with colorful paint sample cards from a hardware store. Yarn, laced through punched holes, joins the cards at the top. At the bottom they are held together with a brass fastener.

Rose-Colored Lorgnette

Multicolored viewer gives you a choice of outlooks. To make one, cut windows in the bumps of half an egg carton. Glue circles of colored cellophane over the windows with rubber cement. Tape on a stick for a holder.

Torn Tissue Design

Torn shapes of bright tissue paper can look spectacular in an abstract design. Arrange the pieces on a sheet of white poster board. Experiment with color mixtures by overlapping some of the pieces—yellow over red creates orange, and pale blue over pink turns into a beautiful shade of violet.

Add a few extra ingredients, like dried weeds or pieces of colored string. Brush white glue, thinned with water, over everything. After the picture dries, you can coat it with glossy acrylic polymer to give it a nice sheen.

Blue Curls

Blue curls can be your crowning glory with a crepe paper wig. Cut a paper plate a little smaller than the crown of your head. Fringe half a roll of crepe paper, cutting parallel to the folds. Unfold the roll and glue the uncut edge to the rim of the circle. Work back and forth, leaving space for your face, until the hair looks thick enough. Use shorter fringes for the top of the wig and for bangs. Make curls by rolling the fringes on a pencil.

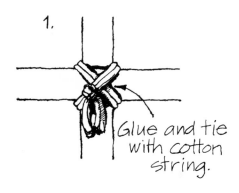

1.

Glue and tie with cotton string.

2.

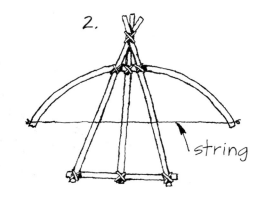

string

Bright Bird Kites

Kite flying is an aerodynamic mystery that you should discuss with your father or mother. While you're at it, ask how to bridle kites and figure out the tails.

Making a kite is something to do on your own while you're waiting for a windy day in March. Hang it on the wall for good luck.

There are fifty to a million different ways to design kites. Here are two paper ones you could try. They're made of bamboo strips joined by white glue and tied string (see sketch 1). Get the bamboo from window shades or from a garden center.

To make the triangular bird kite (sketch 2), join three spine pieces, tepee fashion. Join the straight bottom piece over the spine. The wings are made like an Indian's bow, the tight string making the wood curve. Tie and glue them on last of all.

Sketch 3 shows a more complicated kite pattern. You may have to split the bamboo with heavy scissors to form the bottom loops.

Finish the kites by gluing lightweight tissue or rice paper over the frames (see sketch 4). Decorate them with poster paints. Bits of cloth or crepe paper are good tail material.

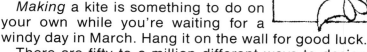

string

3.

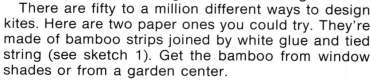

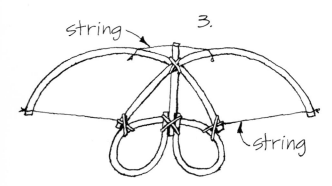

string

4.

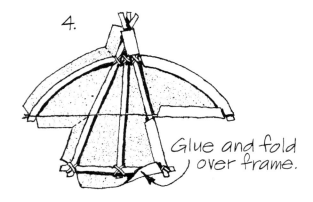

Glue and fold over frame.

Decorated kites make an attractive display on your wall while you wait for March to roll around.

Friendly Faces

Friendly faces flash a smile as you pass by this mobile. They are vinyl color wheels. Cut circles or other shapes from thin vinyl fabric (sold at auto supply stores and upholstery shops).

Using white glue, stick tissue paper to the vinyl. The vinyl will cling to clean window glass, as well as to another piece of vinyl. You can overlap the wheels to experiment with the color spectrum.

For a pretty, translucent mobile, suspend the wheels from a cross made of two sticks tied with string.

When you look at the polka dot fish with your eyes out of focus, he seems to be swimming. You make the dots by using the point and eraser of a pencil instead of a paint brush.

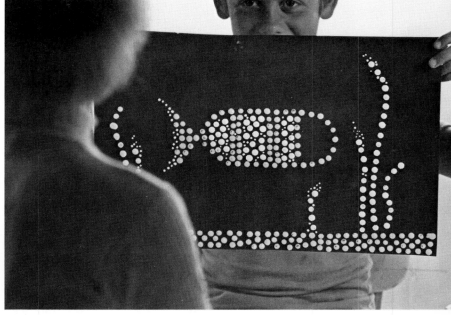

Speckled Paintings

This technique—called pointillism—creates an optical illusion. The picture is composed of dots and specks, but when you stand away from it, they sometimes look like a solid mass of color. If you blur your eyes, the colors seem to dance.

Try your own pointillism with new, sharpened pencils. You'll need one pencil for each color of paint. Draw a picture with a dotted outline lightly in pencil. Dip the erasers and points of the pencils in paint; then stamp them on your paper to cover the pencil dots.

Now squint—you'll be surprised.

Wiggly Self Portraits

The best work space for these is the floor. Lay down three sheets of wrapping paper that are at least as long as you are tall. Tape them together, side by side, using wide gummed mailing tape. (If the tape tastes terrible, you can wet it with a sponge.) Turn the giant piece of paper over.

Next, play some good, lively music. Lie down on the paper and dance. When you get to a pose you like, hold still. Now somebody has to trace all around you with a black crayon—while you try to hold your pose.

Get up and fill in your body outline with color. Paint fancy clothes or a wild costume on your tracing.

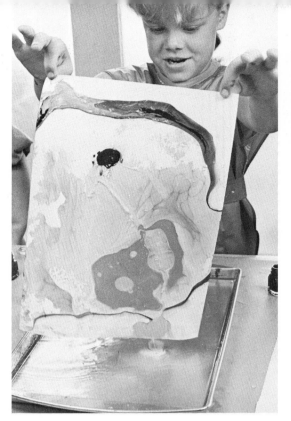

Oil & Water Art

Oil and water have a friendly relationship in a painting. This is how you mix them: partly fill a shallow baking pan with water. Dribble several colors of oil-based enamel paint across the water (it's toxic, so make sure nobody tastes it). Swirl the puddles of paint with a toothpick.

Lay a sheet of good art paper on the surface of the water. Tap it gently; then lift it off and look at the design. Let it dry flat on newspapers (this may take a whole day).

Surprising swirls of color appear when you lift up an oil and water painting.

Shimmer & Shine Wraps

Here is a wonderful way to slap together Christmas wraps in a hurry.

You need a large roll of heavy duty aluminum foil. From an art supply store get some colorful tissue paper and a bottle of glossy acrylic polymer (expensive, but terrific for making things shiny). Mix it with a little water. Tear or cut up the paper. Arrange the pieces on the foil and brush the gloss all over, letting it soak through. Like glue, it makes the paper stick to the foil.

One other nice thing: it's *easy* to wrap packages in foil. You don't even need tape.

Glue bright tissue paper to shiny foil with glossy acrylic polymer. The results are dazzling.

She watches him dash off a 10-finger squiggle. Getting your hands soppy is half the fun of finger painting. See the finger paint recipe on the opposite page.

Friendly beast with a rainbow rib cage is a water color wash. Read about water colors on the opposite page.

Displayed on the refrigerator are a watermark butterfly and a finger painting. Directions for both are given on the opposite page. The oil-and-water painting (top left) is described on page 13, and the crayon-rubbed doilies (top right) on page 7.

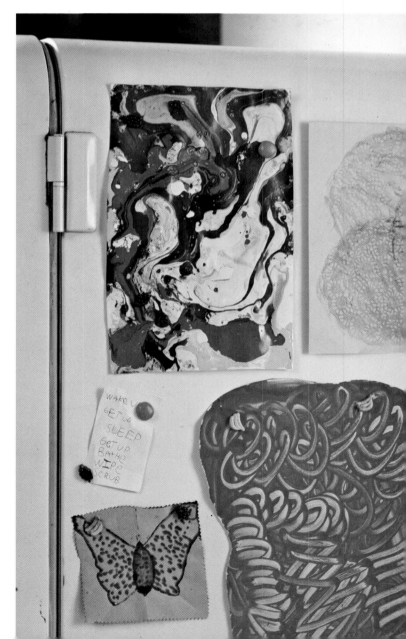

  Paper Play

Finger Paint

Pour a small pool of liquid laundry starch in the middle of some glossy paper. Add some powdered poster paint. Experiment with the amounts of each, mixing with your fingers, until the paint is thick but still runny. Paint with your fingers, fingernails, knuckles, and palms.

You can make a kind of movie with finger paint: work up a design for scene 1; smear it away with your hands and work up a new design for scene 2; continue to the end of the show.

Water Colors

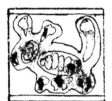

These come in tubes or in tin boxes. Mix water with the paint until it is thin enough to produce bright, watery colors. If you brush water colors over a strong crayon drawing, the drawing will still show through.

Water Dribble Designs

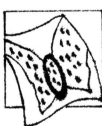

Hold a sheet of construction paper under a running tap. Let the water dribble a design for you. Go over the design with flow pens while the paper is still wet. Try folding the paper in half first to make a water dribble symmetrical print.

Cake Frosting Paint

For a thick, molded painting that looks as if it had been made of cake frosting, mix 1 cup of powdered tempera with 2 tablespoons of wallpaper paste. Add ¼ to ½ cup of liquid laundry starch, mixing until the paint is thick enough to spread like frosting. Use a popsicle stick to model your picture on a piece of white cardboard.

Foot Prints

Lay down a long sheet of wrapping paper or shelf paper (vinyl-coated shelf paper has good skid resistance). Pour poster paint into a metal baking dish big enough for both your feet. Stand in the paint, blot your feet lightly on newspapers, and walk a pattern across the paper.

Tread gently and hold onto someone's hand because this can be slippery. (At the other end of the paper, have a bucket of water and a towel handy.)

Try tennis shoe or galoshes footprints (see page 16).

Sponge Splotches

Use a piece of sponge instead of a brush, one for each color. Dip it in poster paint and experiment on your paper.

Good Impressions

Look around for objects to print with—salt shakers, fly swatters, keys, potato mashers, bottle caps, toy truck wheels, corks, wrenches, or shapes cut from cardboard. Tape whatever it is to a small box, such as a matchbox. Stamp it in poster paint (newspapers make a good ink pad). Then stamp it on paper. If you can carve, try cutting one side of an eraser for block printing. Use a firm rubber one. Draw a picture on it and cut around the edges of the picture to make it stand out. Print with the stamping method described above. (The book covers on the facing page are printed with erasers.)

Tracking blue paint across paper is a little messy, but the results are interesting. Try it in rubber boots, in tennis shoes, or barefoot (see page 15). Cut out the clearest footprints for a wall decoration.

Styrene Foam Print

Green and black angel is a carved block print. Use a block of styrene foam or a supermarket meat tray. A good carving tool is a pencil with a broken lead.

Press down the parts of your design that you do *not* want to print, leaving the rest raised slightly. Roll poster paint on a cookie sheet, using a brayer. Coat the raised parts of the styrene foam with paint. Press paper over it. Lift off your print (this one is black printed on green paper).

Coffee cans, wrapped in hand-printed paper, turn into cheerful cannisters. Read about printing on page 16.

Eraser block prints, described on page 16, become handsome book covers.

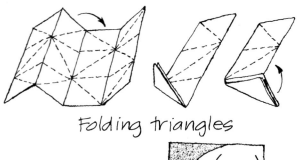

Folding triangles

Dipping

Fold-and-dye is a way of producing colorful patterns on absorbent paper. What you do is fold the paper into a fairly small packet. Experiment with the fold patterns sketched on the left and below, or make up your own.

Dip the corners of the packets in bowls of dye. The dye can be either diluted food coloring or strong water colors. The more absorbent the paper, the faster the dyes will spread. You can control this by blotting the packet between paper towels.

Rice paper takes the dyes beautifully—but this project goes very fast, so you might want to use something less expensive, like paper towels.

Folding squares

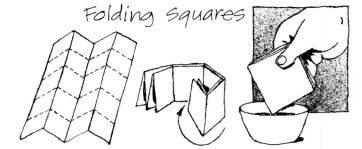

Haiku Books

Cover two squares of cardboard with fold-and-dyed paper. These are the book covers. The inside is a pleated accordion of construction paper. Each end pleat is glued to the inside of the front and back covers.

The accordion can be as long or as short as you like. Fill it with stories, poems, drawings, or whatever you please.

Dip & Dye Snowflakes

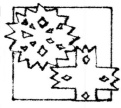

Use cone or square-shaped coffee filter papers. Fold them in half, quarters, thirds—or just fold them haphazardly. Dip them, blot them, open them up, and let them dry. Then fold the papers again. Cut out snowflake lace, following one of the patterns on the left or inventing your own pattern.

Tape the snowflakes to a sunny window —the colors will blaze with holiday cheer.

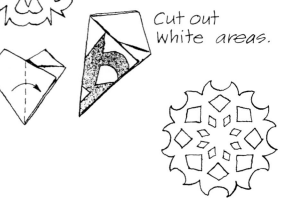

Cut out white areas.

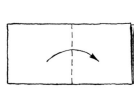

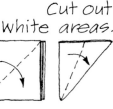

Cut out white areas.

Fold-and-dye craft turns plain rice paper into rainbow-hued gift wrapping paper. Instructions appear on the opposite page.

Snowflakes for all seasons are cut from coffee filter papers. See the opposite page for directions.

Haiku books, filled with poetry, are covered with fold-and-dye paper. They're described on the facing page.

Curly Birds

These are very simple to make. They are curls of construction paper, stapled together. Cut even strips, all the same size. Curl the ends by rolling them up on a pencil. Staple three or four strips together. The curls form the bird's head and tail feathers.

Nestle curly birds in the branches of your Christmas tree or hang them in a mobile.

The Three Penguins

If, when you were very young, you loved the story of the three bears, maybe you'd like to fold a Papa, Mama, and Baby Penguin. Use origami paper from an art supply store or a toy store. Work carefully. Every time you make a fold, go over it with your fingernail so that you make a distinct fold line. Follow the sketches to make penguins of your own.

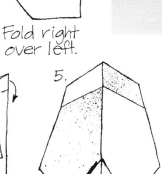

1.
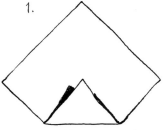
Fold bottom point up to center.

2.
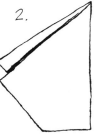
Fold right over left.

3.
Fold triangles on both sides toward center.

4.
Fold top down. Unfold it.

5.
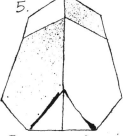
Open up penguin. Fold two sides back again slowly.

6.

...while pushing top point down. Flatten it to form head.

7.

Open wings. Fold triangles toward center. Close wings again.

Origami House

This simple origami project could be used for birthday party place cards. Start by folding a piece of origami paper into quarters. Open up this packet so that you have two halves again. Then follow the sketches below.

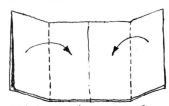

1. Fold right and left quarters to middle. Unfold again.

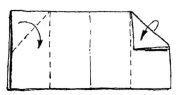

2. Fold right and left top corners down, making triangles. Unfold again.

3. Bring right and left sides to middle again. Open them and squash small triangles to form big ones.

4. Add doors and windows.

Fold-up Puppet

Fold a sheet of construction paper—first into thirds, lengthwise; then into quarters, with the top and bottom meeting in the middle. Fold again in half with the openings on the outside.

Slip your thumb and fingers into the slots to make puppet talk. See page 22 and cover photo.

1. Fold in thirds, lengthwise.

2. Fold in quarters, open ends at the middle.

3. Fold in half, open ends on outside.

4. Glue on features. Slip fingers and thumb into openings.

Pig-unicorn mask with a dreamy expression is formed from construction paper. Read about paper sculpture masks on the facing page; other examples appear on Contents page.

Medieval times come alive with a few toy knights and a paper castle. See directions on the opposite page.

Pretty cardboard cottage makes a perfect sewing box. Directions for making your own are on the facing page.

Talkative rabbit is a folded paper puppet. To learn how to make one, look on page 21. Also, see cover photo.

Stack-together Castle

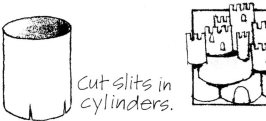

Cut slits in cylinders.

Fit slits together.

This is made of paper cylinders that you stack (see the sketches on the left). Each one has two slits cut halfway through it. The slits interlock, holding the cylinders together. The finished castle is so strong that you can lift it by a turret and it won't fall apart.

Paper Masks

You can make wild, fanciful masks of construction paper by using a few paper sculpture techniques.

First, hold a sheet of paper over your face and have someone lightly mark the positions for your eyes, nose, and mouth. Cut these openings out and draw the basic face you want. You can make it three-dimensional by cutting slits at the chin and sides, and gluing one lap over the other.

Form horns from cones; attach by gluing the overlapping top corner to the face. To make a beak, cut out two triangles, fold them down the center to make them peak, and glue them together.

Attach features neatly by cutting tabs in one end of them (like those on paper doll clothes). Glue the tabs to the inside of the mask. Add whiskers and hair by looping yarn through punched holes.

Decorate with yarn, fringed and curled paper, and punched confetti—you're ready to startle anyone you meet.

Cottage Box

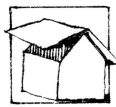

Store your treasures in this handy little cardboard house. One roof flap folds up so you can reach inside.

With pencil and ruler, transfer the patterns on the right to drawing paper. Trace them on lightweight cardboard. Cut out the house and roof, scoring the fold lines so they will bend neatly. Tape or glue the floor and side tabs to the walls. Then attach the remaining tabs (gables and back wall) to half the roof.

Leave the other half open for the box lid. Decorate the cottage with flow pens or paint.

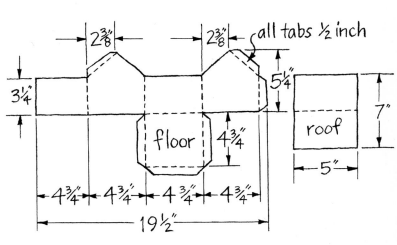

all tabs ½ inch

$2\frac{3}{8}$" $2\frac{3}{8}$" $5\frac{1}{4}$" $3\frac{1}{4}$"

floor $4\frac{3}{4}$"

roof   7"

5"

$4\frac{3}{4}$" $4\frac{3}{4}$" $4\frac{3}{4}$" $4\frac{3}{4}$"

$19\frac{1}{2}$"

Papier-Mâché

These are French words for a special kind of paper modeling. With a thin mixture of flour and water, you paste layers of paper strips over a form. The form can be anything that gives the finished *papier-mâché* the shape you want—for example, crumpled paper, a cardboard tube, or a balloon. For the strips, use newspapers or paper towels, and for a colorful finish, use tissue paper as the final layer. As you paste on the squishy strips, model the form with your fingers.

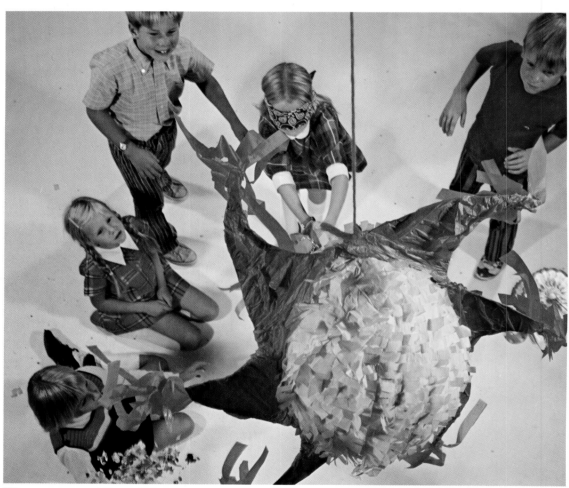

Festive Piñata

Feliz Navidad means Merry Christmas. Maybe it means a piñata, too!

Start with a big balloon hung from a string. Cover the balloon with many layers of paper and paste, leaving a big hole (about 6 inches in diameter) around the string. After this dries (about 2 days), add cardboard cones and fringed crepe paper trim. Pop the balloon and pour in toys and candy.

Fancy Hats

Hats of paper and paste are shaped to fit your own head. Paste together two big squares of wrapping paper. You end up with one damp square. Have somebody set this on your head, mold the crown of the hat, and tie string around your brow to hold the shape. Take it off, shape it, let it dry, and paint it.

Tissue Bracelets

Bangles are papier-mâché molded on cardboard tubes. Tissue paper layers give them brilliant colors.

Paper Menagerie

Colorful animals are papier-mâché molded on forms of crumpled newspaper. Tape on cardboard tubes and other cardboard shapes to make arms, legs, and tails. After painting your animal, you can give him a glossy coat with acrylic polymer.

Big, strong, bold, and friendly—
crocodile, kangaroo, and candy-
striped unicorn are sculptures to ride.

Wild Paper Animals

Building grand-scale, papier-mâché animals on strong frames can give you your own pop art zoo.

The animals on the opposite page were designed by fifth graders. Their fathers helped them build the sturdy wood and chicken wire frames. The unicorn started out as a sawhorse, the kangaroo has a sort of tripod frame inside, and the alligator's skeleton is shown in the photograph on the left.

Each frame is covered with chicken wire, which can be molded and bent to form jaws, ears, camel's humps, and tails.

To give an animal a smooth coat, cover the chicken wire with a layer of aluminum foil. Over this, apply four or five layers of newspaper strips soaked in flour-and-water paste. Model the creature's shape as you work.

It will take several days for the animal to dry. Then you can paint him with acrylics or poster paint to look cheerful or wild or mean. To protect the paint—especially if you're going to ride the beast outside—add a coat of nontoxic varnish.

He bends chicken wire over a plywood frame to construct the alligator's skeleton.

Covering the skeleton with strips of soaking wet newspaper is messy—but it's fun to watch the alligator take shape.

Last of all, paint the creature with bright colors to make him look wild and beautiful.

Knits, Knots & Stitches

Textiles have nice textures. They feel good to touch. Maybe for just this reason, yarn and cloth are especially satisfying to work with. This chapter will go into interesting kinds of finger work with different textiles—winding, weaving, knotting, knitting, stitching, and twisting.

Gather up an assortment of yarn, fabric scraps, felt squares, twine, rope, and trimmings. Buy remnants at yardage shops, looking particularly for cloth with pleasing patterns and textures. Save soft rags for stuffing or buy a bag of polyester stuffing at a dime store. Maybe you know someone who would give you leftover yarn from knitting. You'll also need a pin cushion, some big needles, and good scissors (left-handed, if you are).

Put everything in a box or basket, and you'll be all set to enjoy the projects on the coming pages.

Ojos de Dios

These are Spanish words for "eyes of God," pronounced ohos day *dee* os. They are colorful diamonds of yarn wound on crossed sticks.

Cross two sticks (popsicle sticks, chopsticks, dowels, or branches). Bind them with crisscrossed yarn, wrapped several times over. Form the diamond by wrapping the yarn once around each arm of the cross. Vary the colors as you go, so you work up a nice pattern. When you decide the diamond is big enough, tie off the end of the yarn.

Tie tassles to the ends of the sticks—or, for more elaborate *ojos de Dios,* tie small crossed sticks to each point of the cross and wind miniature yarn diamonds on them.

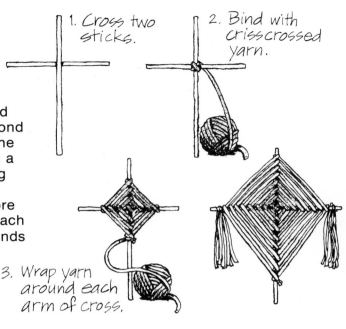

1. Cross two sticks.

2. Bind with crisscrossed yarn.

3. Wrap yarn around each arm of cross.

Felt Doll

This doll acts like a paper doll, but its clothes are made of cloth. They stick to the doll's felt body.

With flow pens, draw a person on a felt square. Have the arms held away from the body. Glue the felt to cardboard, cut out the doll, and glue on yarn hair.

To make the clothing, trace around the body with flow pens on fabric scraps. Cut out the clothes and dress up your doll.

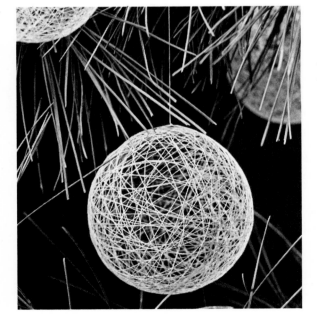

Lacy Thread Balls

These light, delicate ornaments are nothing but thread and air. You make them by wrapping balloons with thread that has been soaked in starch.

Lay a spool of thread on its side in a small bowl; cover it completely with liquid starch. Hang a small balloon over the bowl and wind the thread around it firmly (not too tightly, or you might pop the balloon). Keep winding until the balloon is covered with a fine network of thread, like a cobweb. Then cut the end of the thread and smooth it down. Let the starch dry overnight; then pop the balloon and gently remove it.

Hang lace balls on your Christmas tree or in a window.

Shape your tapestry to suit your fancy. A cardboard tube can become a muff, napkin ring, bracelet—or just a nicely decorated cardboard tube. Details are given on the opposite page.

Weave boldly striped head band with three colors of yarn over drinking straws. Directions are given on the opposite page.

Fork weaving is a good way to pass the time while you're waiting for supper. Try weaving on other things, like a berry basket, bike wheel, or badminton net.

This warm and cheery tapestry was woven by a group of boys and girls. Everyone put in his favorite color. Quite often it was red. Windows were created by separating the warp threads with narrow rows of woof.

1. String warp tightly.

2. Weave over and under with woof.

3. Tighten rows with fork.

4. Hang after threading dowels through end loops of warp.

Warp & Woof

Weaving is a way of locking threads together. It happens when horizontal ones cross over and under vertical ones. The vertical threads are called *warp;* the horizontal ones are called *woof.*

The warp should be straight, tightly strung, and spaced as evenly as possible. Use something strong for it, like twine. The woof is much freer. Keep it loose so it doesn't pull the tapestry out of shape.

You can begin and end the woof almost anywhere. Tie off the loose ends or tuck them into the material you've already woven. Pack down rows of woof with a fork or a comb.

Yarn is a wonderful woof material for tapestries that are warm and soft to touch. Also try fabric strips, rolled cotton wool, ribbons, jute, or any long, stringy material that appeals to you.

Before you can weave, you need some kind of frame. An old picture frame, studded along two ends with nails, is perfect. String the warp between the nails.

A nice way to hang a woven tapestry is to thread branches or dowels between the loops at the top and bottom ends of the warp.

Cardboard Tapestries

For a very simple loom, cut slots in two ends of an oblong-shaped piece of thick cardboard. Space the slots evenly. String the warp between the slots and start weaving. When you're finished, cut and tie off the warp at each end.

For more interesting shapes, try the same thing with a piece of cardboard tube, or use a sturdy paper plate. Thread wire through loops at the ends of the warp to hold the shape.

Indian Head Band

This can also be a belt or a jingle bell strap. Cut four lengths of twine, 36 inches long. Thread each through a drinking straw. Divide the twine into pairs, knot them together, and loop the knot over a door knob or chair back. (See the sketch on the right.) Push the straws against the knot. Weave yarn over and under them until they're covered; then push the woven material toward the knot and pull the straws toward you.

Keep weaving in this fashion until your band is as long as you need it. Remove straws. Knot the twine at both ends to hold the yarn in place.

Weave over and under drinking straws.

Floppy patchwork marionette dances as you bounce him on elastic strings. Read on the opposite page about how to make your own puppet.

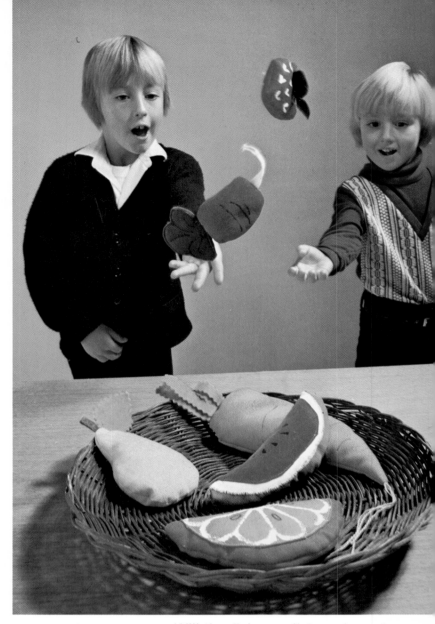

Will the flying radish and soaring strawberry land in the basket? Like the pear, carrot, watermelon and orange slices, they're painted bean bags. Read on the opposite page about turning your favorite food into a tossing toy.

Glove Family

One pair of gloves will yield 10 little puppet heads. You stuff a cotton ball into each finger and tie it in place with string. Sew on beads, sequins, and bits of felt for faces. A few loose stitches of yarn will give each head a hairdo.

Bean Bag Food

Cotton carrots, potatoes, and apples are good for tossing around between meals or even for playing indoor basketball.

Draw a simple picture of your favorite food. Cut it out and pin it to two layers of cloth. Cut out the cloth pieces; then paint details on the front and back (or use a black flow pen).

With the right sides together, stitch the front to the back, leaving 2 inches open. Make short, tightly spaced stitches to be sure the beans won't leak out. Turn the bag right side out and fill it with rice or beans. Tuck in the raw edges and sew up the opening.

If leaves would make the food more realistic, they can be cut out of felt and stitched on last of all.

Patchwork Puff Puppet

Use up small fabric scraps to create this multicolored marionette. He's made of circles that are gathered around the edge so they puff. For long, floppy arms and legs, he needs lots of circles, so this project may take you several afternoons.

Cut paper patterns for a 4-inch circle and an 8-inch circle. The smaller circles form the arms and legs. These can be as long as you like—maybe 12 for each arm and 24 for each leg. That adds up to 72 circles! But you can pin your pattern to three or four layers of fabric and cut them all out at once. Cut out six to eight big circles for the body, the head, and a cap.

Gather the edges of each circle with a running stitch (see the sketches on the left). Pull the gathers tight, to make the circles puff; then knot the thread. (For the head, add stuffing before you tighten the gathers.)

String the arm and leg circles on thin elastic cord. Stack the body circles, sewing them together through their centers. Stitch the arms, legs, and head to the body. Add the cap and a button and felt face.

Sew long pieces of elastic cord to the marionette's hands, feet, and cap. Attach the cords to a dowel or a chopstick. Wiggle the stick to make the puppet dance.

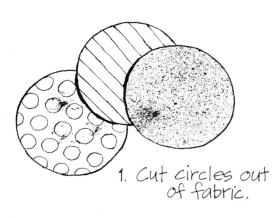

1. Cut circles out of fabric.

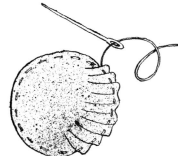

2. Gather the edge with a running stitch.

3. Pull stitches tight to make circle puff.

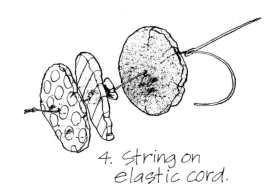

4. String on elastic cord.

Sunshine Banner

The colors in this banner gradually come to life as the sun warms them up.

You'll need a few supplies from an art store for this project. Ask for several colors of dyes that develop in the sun and for a jar of "resist" (a paste that blocks out the areas you don't want to dye).

Make a simple drawing with the resist on plain, untreated cotton. (An easy way to do this is to squeeze the resist out of a plastic catsup bottle.) Brush the dyes over the drawing. Lay the cloth in the sunshine for about half an hour and watch the colors emerge. After they ripen fully, wash the banner in warm, soapy water to remove the resist.

Fabric Paint

Use this special paint to turn plain T-shirts and jeans into brilliant works of art—or to design mural curtains for your bedroom. You can buy it at art supply stores (be sure to get the water-based kind). Practice with sketches before you start painting on cloth. To set the colors permanently—after the paint is dry—put the cloth in a drier for 45 minutes.

Launder fabric-painted materials in cold water with mild detergent.

Tie-and-fade can produce a sunburst of brilliant streaks, and every pattern is different. It all depends on where you tie the cloth.

Tie & Fade

To design striking place mats or to decorate blue jeans, try this simple technique. Tying creates a pattern, and fading removes color so the pattern will show up.

Use cotton of any dark shade that has not been given a permanent finish. The fading takes place when the cloth is soaked in a solution of half water and half chlorine bleach. (If you're fading blue jeans, use a weaker solution.) The tied parts of the cloth stay dark; the rest fades to various lighter shades.

Bleach can hurt your eyes, so be careful not to splash.

Take time to experiment with the many ways to fold and tie. For stripes, fold accordion pleats and tie at intervals. For a sunburst, hold the cloth by the center and tie it just the way it hangs—in three or four places.

When you dunk the cloth, its dyes react chemically with the bleach. This makes the solution heat up, so wear rubber gloves to protect your hands. Let the tied cloth soak for a few minutes. Then remove it and rinse under cold water. Untie it, rinse again, and hang it up to dry.

How many imaginative ways can you think of to use tie-and-fade?

Her T-shirt makes an important announcement. Spot will be very pleased to hear it. Like the fanciful mural curtains below, it's decorated with fabric paint. Directions are given on the opposite page.

Like magic, the sun developed the colors in her clown banner. Look on the opposite page to see how to make one of your own.

Trio of friends sharing the armchair are fabric-painted dolls. Outline the doll's front on paper. Pin this pattern to two thicknesses of cloth. Cut out, leaving an extra inch all around for a seam. Paint both sides (see opposite page—fabric paint), stitch, and stuff.

Let your imagination wander. All kinds of creatures—real or fanciful—can be made of rope. How about a toothy alligator—or a snake to scare your sister?

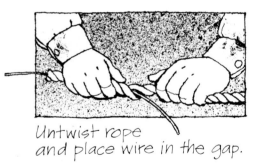

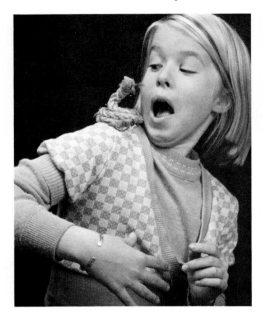

Untwist rope and place wire in the gap.

Tie on legs.

Twisted Rope Creatures

You and your friends can make a wild menagerie with a few hardware store supplies and trimmings you probably already have at home. You'll need ¼ or ½-inch hemp rope, cut in lengths of 15 inches. To shape the rope into an animal form, use wire and wire cutters.

Cut the wire to the same length as the rope pieces. (Handle the wire cutters with care.) Straighten the pieces of wire, if necessary. Threading them into the rope takes a little patience (see the sketch on the left).

First, you untwist the hemp just a little, making a gap in the rope. Place the wire diagonally along the gap. Let the rope spring back into shape; this holds the wire in place. Keep working this way along the length of the rope.

You can make a four-legged friend with three pieces of wired rope. Bend a long piece to form a head, body, and tail. Fold two shorter pieces to make pairs of legs (see the sketch on the left). Tie the legs to the body with crisscrossed string.

To achieve shaggy manes and tails, unravel the hemp, pulling apart its fibers. Tie off with string. Bind cut ends—the animal's feet, for example—to keep them from unravelling.

If you want your animal to be colorful, dip him in a bath of water colors or food coloring. Let him dry completely before you add trim.

Look around for trimmings to improve your creature's looks. Glue on beads, buttons, bottle caps, corks. Felt is good for teeth, ribbon and braid for saddles and reins.

Jute Dolls

Wound and twisted jute dolls have multiple joints. You can bend them any which way—to sit in funny positions, climb trees, dance, or steer a truck. Make a whole family of them for your doll house.

Jute dolls can be of any size, depending on the length of the four starting cords. Besides jute, you can make them of heavy twine or rug yarn. You'll need two macramé pins (or any pin with a large head) and a board or piece of sturdy cardboard to work on. After the doll is finished, you can glue on yarn hair, felt features, and fabric scrap clothing.

Cut four cords, each 24 inches long. Fold them in half; then hang them from the center over one of the pins stuck in the board. Cut another cord 8 inches long. Fold one end of it back, pinning the fold next to the other cords.

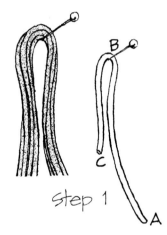

Step 1

Wrap end A tightly around all the other cords just above end C. This forms the doll's neck. To finish, thread end A through loop B. Remove the pin from loop B. Pull end C down firmly, making a knot around end A. Cut off the loose ends.

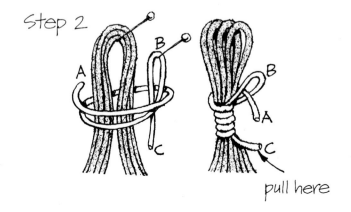

Step 2

pull here

Take the two outside cords on both sides to form arms. Cut two cords, each 10 inches long. Fold them at one end and pin them on either side, next to the arm cords. Start at the hand and wrap up to the neck, the same way you wrapped the neck.

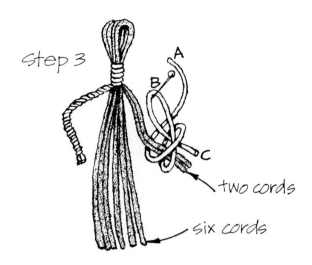

Step 3

A

B

C

two cords

six cords

If you like, you can change colors to wrap the doll's body. Cut a 20-inch cord. Wrap the six center cords, starting at the hips and working up to the neck.

Each leg is three cords. Divide them and wrap from the feet up to the body.

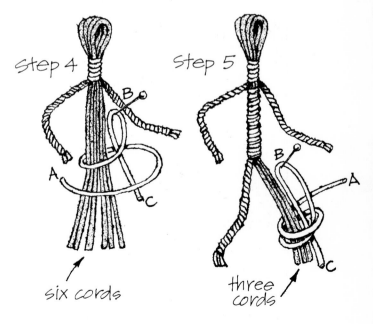

Step 4

B

A

C

six cords

Step 5

B

A

C

three cords

Soft and squeezy doll is made of cotton socks. You cut, stuff, and stitch one pair. Look on opposite page to see how to make a cuddly sock doll of your own.

Felt friends are fun to design, simple to sew. You can make a pile of them in one afternoon to give away or to sit on your bed. They're described on the opposite page.

Scary Harry and Smiley Giles are felt glove puppets. They're easy to sew even if you've never used a needle and thread before. The pattern for them is a tracing of your hand. Directions are given on the opposite page.

Felt Friends

These dolls, made from felt squares, are easy as pie to put together.

Pin two squares of felt together. Cut curves out of the two top corners to create a rounded head shape. Unpin the two pieces; sew felt features on one of them. Cut straight arms and legs from two layers of felt. Stitch the layers together along the edges. Make ears and horns the same way.

Stitch together the doll's front and back about ¼ inch from the outside edges. Leave the bottom edge open for stuffing and adding legs. Leave small openings where you can later add arms, yarn hair, ears, or horns.

Stuff the doll, poking the ends of arms, legs, ears, and hair in the openings as you go. Sew all openings closed.

Harry & Giles

Pin two felt squares together. Lay your hand on top with your thumb and little finger spread apart. Trace your hand, keeping your pen about an inch away all the way around. Cut along this line. Finish the puppet just as if he were a felt friend, only leave the bottom edge open like a glove.

Cotton Sock Dolls

If you're rapidly outgrowing your socks—but not wearing holes in them—save them for dolls. Otherwise, buy plain, colored, or fancy socks at the dime store.

The toe becomes a round head; the heel is shaped to make a plump rear end so your doll can sit easily. The ribbed ankle is cut down the middle for legs (very long legs if you use knee socks). The other sock provides arms and knitted clothing.

Look at the sketches on the right to see how you cut the socks. Stuff the foot of one sock to make the doll's body. If you want it to have a small, round nose, put a bean between the sock and the stuffing where a nose would be. Stitch around the bean to outline it.

Give the doll a neck by tying string, like a necklace, just below the chin. Sew up the leg seams, tucking the raw edges inside. Leave openings so you can add stuffing. Sew them closed afterwards. Arms are made like the legs, from the ribbing of the other sock, and stitched in place.

After the doll is sewn together, add loops of yarn or frayed jute for hair. To give it a special personality, add button eyes and felt or flow pen features.

1. Cut ribbing of one sock to form legs.

Cut off ribbing of the other sock for arms.

2. Stuff sock. Then stitch leg seams.

3. Stuff and stitch arms. Then sew to body.

Rope & Yarn Basket

You can make your own basket for Easter or daily egg gathering. All you need is about one yard of rope and assorted colors of yarn.

Bend back one end of the rope about an inch and tie it firmly with a 12-inch length of yarn (see the sketches below). Thread the other end of the yarn through a large tapestry needle. Gradually coil the rope to form the flat basket bottom. As you do this, bind the coils with yarn stitches.

Loop the first stitch around two coils. Loop the next few stitches (about ½ inch) around only the *outside* coil. Then bind two coils again.

Continue this pattern as you shape the coils on top of each other to form the basket sides. Tie on new yarn of different colors as you go. Leave some rope free for a handle. Wrap it with yarn and sew its end firmly to the rim of the basket.

1.
Bend back 1 inch of rope and tie. Bind 2 rows together.

2.
Wrap outside row several times.

3.
Every ½ inch, bind 2 rows together.

1. Wrap yarn around nails.

2. Wrap a second row.

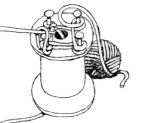

3. With needle, lift bottom loop over nail.

4.
Pull down to tighten stitch.

Spool Knitting

This is a very simple, time-honored way to knit a cord. You need a ball of yarn, a large wood spool, four round-headed nails, and a tapestry needle.

Hammer the nails into one end of the spool, spacing them evenly around the center hole. Unwind 6 inches of yarn. Drop this length through the hole at the nailed end of the spool. Unwinding a little more yarn, loop it around each nail in turn, starting from the inside (see the sketches on the left).

Push the yarn down to the base of the nails. When all four nails are wrapped, go around them again the same way. You end up with two rows of yarn.

Hook the tapestry needle through the bottom row on the outside of one of the nails. Pull this strand of yarn over the nail to the inside.

When you've done this on all four nails, pull on the yarn hanging through the bottom of the spool. Now you've made one stitch.

If you make 100—or 1,000—more like it, a long, thin cord of knitting will result. The uses of the cord are up to your imagination.

Embroidered Bean Bags

Make a batch of these charming bean bags for gifts or party favors. Decorate them with fancy stitches.

Using about half a sheet of 8 by 10-inch paper, draw a simple shape or animal. Pin this pattern to two layers of plain, soft cloth. Cut out the bean bag's front and back.

Make stitches with yarn or embroidery floss on the front piece. The sketches below show a few you might like to try. To add more color, sew on pieces of felt.

Sew the front to the back, right sides together, leaving a 3-inch opening. Use small, tightly spaced stitches. Turn the bag right side out again and fill it with rice or beans. Sew the opening closed at least twice to avoid leaks.

You can have fun tossing your bean bag—or using it as a paper weight.

Chain Stitch: Come up at A. Form loop and hold with your thumb. Go in next to A. Come up at B.

Cross Stitch: Make a row of diagonal stitches. Cross with diagonal stitches going the opposite way.

Blanket Stitch: Come up at A. Go in at B, leaving a small loop. Come up again at C.

Stitchery Bags

Burlap and heavy yarn are good materials to work with if you're trying embroidery for the first time. Use enough cloth to double over for a drawstring bag.

Draw a picture on the front of the bag with chalk. Go over the chalk lines with stitches. The chain stitch, shown above, makes a nice, thick line.

Sew up the sides of the bag, right sides together. Hem the opening, leaving space to insert a drawstring.

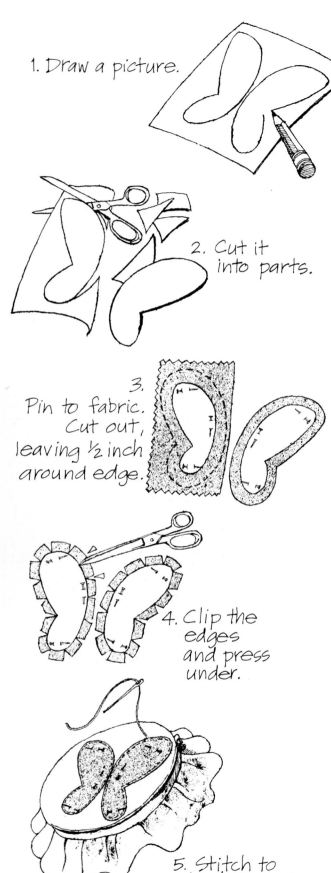

1. Draw a picture.

2. Cut it into parts.

3. Pin to fabric. Cut out, leaving ½ inch around edge.

4. Clip the edges and press under.

5. Stitch to background.

Friendship Quilt

Making a quilt is often the cooperative venture of friends who get together at a party called a "quilting bee." It's more fun to work this way, and the quilt goes together very fast.

There are many different ways to quilt. For your first quilting bee, you might like to try the appliqué technique shown on the opposite page. Each person designs an appliqué scene on one square of the quilt. Afterwards, the squares are arranged on a background, creating a kind of picture gallery.

Appliqué, in sewing, means stitching pieces of fabric to a contrasting background. First, the raw edges are tucked under and pressed. Then the pieces are pinned in place. It's easier to stitch them if you stretch the background fabric in an embroidery hoop. If you don't do this, try to keep the fabric smooth with your hand as you work.

All the background pieces should be the same size—about 10 inches square. Pick solid colors so the appliqué will show up clearly.

Draw a simple picture on paper. Make it something you can cut into parts, like a triple-scoop ice cream cone. Pin each part of your picture to a fabric scrap. Cut out the pieces, leaving a ½-inch hem all around for tucking under.

Put your appliqué picture together just like a puzzle. Pin the pieces to the center area of the quilt square. Sew along the hemmed edges, using a running stitch or fancy embroidery (see page 41 for sketches of fancy stitches).

When everyone's square is finished, the quilt can be put together on a sewing machine. Have someone help you. You need two large, oblong pieces of fabric for the front and back of the quilt.

Arrange the appliqué squares evenly on the front. Mark their positions with pins. Pressing under the raw edges of each square, pin the squares in place and stitch them to the background.

Baste rolled quilt stuffing to the wrong side of the front piece. Stitch the front to the back, right sides together, leaving one end open. Turn right side out, press, and hem the opening closed.

Now the quilt is finished—though, if you like, you can stitch through all thicknesses to outline each square.

A quilt to treasure was produced when 24 fourth graders combined their talents. Each person designed one square. See the opposite page for details on making your own appliqué quilt.

Ragbraid Purse

If you can braid pigtails, you can make a colorful ragbraid shoulder bag like this one.

Use narrow 36-inch strips of fabric. Press under the raw edges and fold them in half. Sew three strips together at one end. Attach this end to the back of a chair and braid. When you've braided to the end of the first three strips, sew on new ones.

The size of your bag depends on the length of braid; 7 yards went into this one. When you have about that amount braided, cut the length in half. Lay one half flat on a table, wrong side up. Coil it, pin it, and stitch the rows together. Leave about 30 inches loose for a shoulder strap. Sew the far end of the strap 8 inches from the near end.

Make the second side of the bag as you did the first. Stitch the two sides together, leaving the bag open on top between the ends of the shoulder strap.

Scraps & Things

This chapter takes you on a treasure hunt. To be a good hunter, all you need are wit, curiosity, and sharp eyes. Look for stuff that sparks your imagination and that, with a little tinkering, you could transform, or add to something.

You probably already have plenty of usable junk at home—corks, bottle caps, spools, wire, milk and egg cartons, scrap lumber, and hardware. Ask neighbors if you can clean out their garages and basements in exchange for a few craft supplies. To uncover other treasure, you and your parents can explore garage sales and flea markets, building sites, commercial trash bins, and the city dump.

The projects on the pages ahead will give you ideas on how to turn your junk into games, gadgets, toys, and works of art.

Miniature Buildings

Decorative molding (used to make furniture and picture frames) comes in a variety of fancy shapes. The scraps can be glued together to form imaginative miniature buildings. Check with a cabinet maker or frame shop to see if you can salvage some of their leftovers. Otherwise, you can buy molding by the foot at lumber yards.

Cut the scraps into short pieces with a handsaw. Smooth rough edges with sandpaper. Study the shapes to decide what sort of building (or part of a building) they suggest. Join the pieces with white glue. Let the miniature buildings dry overnight; then you can paint them or add details with flow pens.

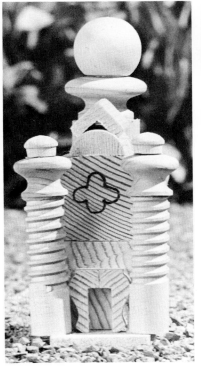

Wood Scrap Sculpture

Wherever carpenters are working on a house, you can gather odd scraps of lumber for sculpture. Ask if you can clean up the building site; the builders will probably be grateful for your help. You'll find boxfuls of small squares, triangles, and odd shapes. Save big scraps to cut up later with a handsaw.

When you've collected a good assortment, construct the sculpture by joining miniature blocks with white glue. Sand the blocks lightly. Make a fairly wide, solid base to help keep your structure from toppling as it grows. Using plenty of white glue, press each block firmly in place. Hold it for a minute or two to let the glue set. Let the sculpture dry overnight.

They're getting acquainted with a junk robot. Weird-looking, he's really harmless—just cardboard and batteries. Details are given on the next page.

Cheerful houses, stores, and churches invite you to visit this model town. You can design your own with grocery cartons—see the opposite page.

Periscopes let you see high up, low down, sideways, or out front. Look on the opposite page for directions.

Robert Robot

You can create a robot companion—or a monster or creature from outer space—with a few boxes, big cardboard tubes, and tape. For strong joints use heavy cloth tape, such as wide adhesive tape or electrical tape.

Use cardboard tubes or small boxes for arms and legs. Stand the legs in a large box full of gravel to keep the robot's balance steady. Attach arms and legs to a large carton body by cutting holes in the carton, inserting the limbs, and taping the joints. A smaller carton provides his head.

Cover the robot with aluminum foil—or paint him. Tape and glue on junk for such special gadgets as a control panel and antennae. To add splendor give him flashlight eyes.

Give Robert a voice by putting a transistor radio or tape recorder inside.

Grocery Carton Town

If you collect plenty of sturdy cardboard cartons, you can design the kind of town you'd most like to live in. Cartons can be easily transformed into houses, stores, restaurants, schools, churches, and apartment buildings—even into a city of the future.

Sketch your town on paper before you start working on the boxes.

Draw windows and doors on the boxes and cut them out with sharp scissors (or a craft knife, if you're used to handling one). Cut up a few extra boxes for roof tops and trees. Using wide mailing tape or masking tape, attach two box sides to make a pitched roof. Use the same tape to attach roofs to box buildings. Cut out cardboard trees and tripod bases for them. Cut a slot in the center of each base so you can poke the trunk inside.

To make the buildings attractive, decorate them with poster paint and glued-on tissue paper. Arrange the town on a pretty, green lawn.

Periscope

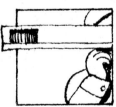

Periscopes are good for spying. They let you peek over fences, glance around trees, or peer down at the sidewalk from a balcony. To construct one, you need a narrow box no longer than 3 feet (a shoe box will do), two metal mirrors from a sporting goods store, and some masking tape.

Place one of the mirrors on the bottom of one side of the box. Trace around it. Do the same on the top of the other side of the box.

The sketches on the right show how to fix the mirrors in place. You will probably have to adjust one of them to make the periscope work properly. You'll know it's working when you can see out of the top hole by looking through the bottom hole.

To finish up, put the lid on the box. Then seal the edges with masking tape and paint the box.

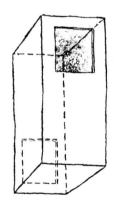

1. Cut two windows in a long box as shown.

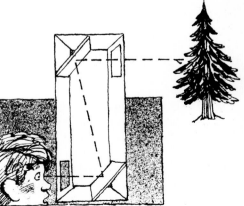

2. Glue mirrors inside as shown. When you look through bottom window you can see out the top.

Cardboard Kachinas

Collect assorted paper towel, toilet paper, and mailing tubes—or make tubes by rolling and taping corrugated cardboard. Save up some dry cleaners' hangers that have thin cardboard tubes on them. Find some beautiful feathers. Now you have the basic materials to make your own Hopi Kachina spirit dolls.

The library should have books with pictures of these dolls to help you make authentic-looking ones.

Cut the big tubes into various lengths, using a small handsaw, or a serrated bread knife. These sections will be the bodies. For arms, use narrow cardboard tubes from dry cleaners' metal hangers. If you want to paint a cardboard tube some lively color, do this and hang it to dry before you untwist the hanger. Remove the tube for cutting into arms.

Cut out tube legs or paint them on. Attach arms and features with sturdy straight pins. After painting and drying the dolls, add feathers with white glue.

Your Hopi dolls will add a real American Indian flavor to your collection.

Rubber Band Board

This simple game is handy for passing the time on a long car trip. You loop rubber bands of different colors and sizes around nails hammered in a board. Two people can play a game by trying to cover the board with triangles that don't overlap.

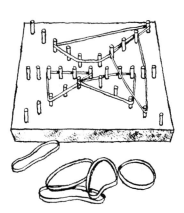

Use a board that's at least ¾ inch thick and 10 or 12 inches square. Mark a geometric pattern of dots—such as a star with eight points—and hammer finishing nails through the dots (see the sketch on the right).

Hardware Design

With some rough wood and assorted hardware, you can hammer together a good-looking outdoor sculpture. Its colors and textures will improve with plenty of wind and rain. In time, ungalvanized nails rust to a rich bronze color; galvanized ones stay dull gray.

Trace a simple design on unfinished cedar or redwood. Outline it with different sizes of nails, washers, staples, and odd metal scraps.

The owl on the left has a curtain rod holder for a nose. His washer eyes are circled with furniture tacks. Spikes hammered at a sharp angle form a ruff of feathers around his neck, and plain roofing nails outline his body.

Ring & Pin

Some folk toys appear in different cultures all around the world. American Indian women have used this simple game of skill for gambling. You toss a string of rings into the air and see how many you can catch on a stick.

Make it with whatever you have on hand. A dowel, an unsharpened pencil, or a whittled branch will do for the pin. Find four or five curtain rings, canning jar rings, or binder rings to string on about a 14-inch length of twine. Tie one end of the twine to the last ring and the other end to the bottom of the stick.

Then toss it and try your luck.

Portrait Doll

This life-size doll can be a portrait of you—or it can be just a friend to sit in a chair, fooling people. At first glance, they'll think it's a real person. Put it together with your outgrown clothes. A styrene foam wig head stuck inside the neck of your old shirt provides the doll's head. For hair, use a clean cotton mop or unravelled rope. Add a few special touches like an old pair of ice skates, sun glasses, and an eye-catching hat.

Stuff each article of clothing until it's fat and firm. Use gloves for hands, socks for feet. Stitch everything together with strong thread or dental floss. Cover stitches around the waist with a belt or sash.

Paint the wig head. (If you want to change the features, carve it first.) Push its neck deep inside the stuffed shirt and tie it in place tightly with string.

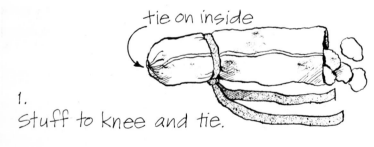

tie on inside

1. Stuff to knee and tie.

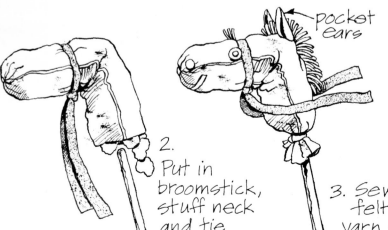

pocket ears

2. Put in broomstick, stuff neck and tie.

3. Sew on felt and yarn features.

Flea Market Costumes

For Halloween, a masquerade, a drama, or just for the joy of it, something magical happens when you dress up in costume.

You can invent an elaborate get-up from odds and ends. To start, spend an adventurous day with your parents looking for finery at flea markets, garage sales, thrift stores, and rummage sales.

Curtains and tablecloths—with a little cutting and folding—can become shawls and capes. Fancy hats with feathers, flowers, or veils can be left alone, transformed, or taken apart for raw materials. A few scarves and some jewelry turn ordinary people into gypsies and pirates.

All you really need, besides these easy-to-find materials, are some imagination and safety pins.

Blue Jeans Hobby Horse

Maybe you're taller than your jeans and want to make cut-offs. And maybe you have a small brother, sister, cousin, or friend in need of a hobby horse. If so, save the pant legs, find an old broom stick, and make a blue jeans bronco.

Following the sketches on the left, turn one leg inside out and tie its cut end tightly closed. Turn it right side out again. Stuff it to the knee and tie it with wide ribbon, leaving long ends of ribbon for reins. Stick the broomstick into the part of the leg that's left over. Stuff all around the stick to fatten the horse's neck—and tie again with ribbon.

Sew on ears made of folded jeans pockets. Add a mane and features of yarn, felt, or blue jean scraps. Now you're ready to gallop away.

Star spangled soldier and stylishly turned-out lady parade their flea market finery. Other costume suggestions are given on the opposite page.

Dressed in your clothes and wearing your father's old hat, he looks like a real person. Really he's a life-size portrait doll, described on the opposite page.

Young cowboy enjoys a wild ride on his denim bronco, made from a stuffed and tied blue jeans leg. See the opposite page for directions.

Plastic Boats

Styrene foam is light and seaworthy. Starting with a thick block for a hull, you can construct all different kinds of vessels with it. The design depends on your imagination, the kind of boat you want to build, and what kinds of plastic scraps you have on hand.

You can carve the hull easily with a jackknife. Make cabins from smaller pieces of styrene foam, parts of egg cartons, coffee cups, and berry baskets. Glue them in place with rubber cement.

Straight branches, popsicle sticks, or thin dowels will serve as masts. Dab a little rubber cement on the end of the mast and poke it into the hull. Cut out sails from heavy paper or styrene foam meat trays and glue them to the masts.

Last of all, add a rigging of string and decorations of assorted junk—bottle caps, corks, buttons, or whatever you can find.

Tie a long string to your craft before you sail it to be sure it doesn't float away.

Inner Tube Raft

For a summer full of wet adventures, assemble this simple, inexpensive raft. Paddle it across a lake, pole your way down a creek, or float it in a swimming pool.

All you need to make one are three inner tubes, 30 feet of nylon rope, and a board that's as long as the inner tubes lined up. You'll have to use a drill and handsaw; ask for help if you need it.

Line up the inner tubes. Lay the board across their tops. With the handsaw, round the corners of the board to prevent sharp bumps when you fall off the raft. Allow no more than 6 inches to hang over the inner tubes at each end. Remove splinters from the board and sand rough edges. You may want to paint your board a brilliant color.

To mark where to drill the holes, lay the inner tubes on top of the board. Keep the marks 1 inch from the edge of the board. (See the sketches below.) Lace rope through the holes, tying the ends so that the inner tubes are fastened securely to the board.

Climb aboard for a floating good time.

Bottom View

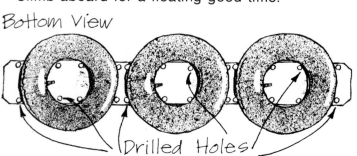

Drilled Holes

Side View

Laced rope

Flying Lunch Bag

This simple kite is a redesigned paper grocery or lunch bag. The only other materials you need are a ball of cotton string and some tape.

Make an open sleeve by cutting off the bottom.

On the seam side of the sleeve, mark point A in the center, ⅓ of the way down from the top. Stick a cross of tape over this mark. Mark four points ¼ inch in from each corner of the bag. Draw lines from these marks to the crossed tapes. Cut out wings along these lines through the top side of the bag only (see sketch 1).

Spread the wings, turn the bag over, and tape the wings to the body.

Cut out a triangular vent, taping corners for strength. Cross tape and punch holes at point B (see sketch 2).

Cut a 6-foot length of string for a bridle. Tie each end through the holes at point B. Tie a loop in the center of the string; attach the loop to a flying line wound on a stick.

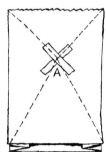

1. Cut along dotted lines this side only.

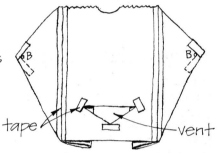

tape

vent

2. Turn over and tape.

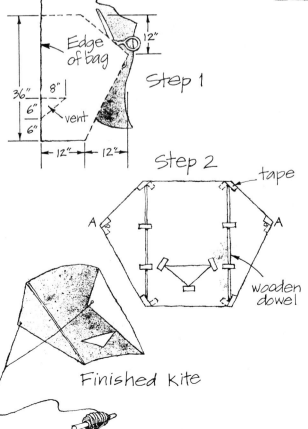

Edge of bag

12"

Step 1

36" 8"

6"

6"

vent

12" 12"

Step 2

tape

A   A

wooden dowel

Finished Kite

Garbage Can Liner Kite

Plastic is perfect kite material, light enough to fly even in a lazy breeze.

Use a bag that's at least 24 by 36 inches. (You could substitute a plastic sheet that measures at least 36 by 48 inches.) You also need two 3-foot lengths of ³⁄₁₆-inch dowels, some tape, and a ball of cotton string.

Spread the bag flat. Transfer the cutting pattern shown in sketch 1, marking the bag with a flow pen. Cut through both thicknesses along the top and right sides. Cut out the triangular vent in the left side. Unfold the bag.

Tape on the dowels as in sketch 2: twice in the middle and at either end (wrap tape over the dowel ends). Tape the corners of the vent to prevent tearing. Fold strips of tape over the wing tips and punch holes for the bridle at point A.

Cut a 10-foot length of string for a bridle, tying each end through the holes at point A. Tie a loop in the center of the bridle and attach a flying line to this point.

Radiant Christmas lanterns are really humble tin cans. You punch out designs with a hammer and nail and then light a candle inside to make the pattern glow (see instructions on the next page).

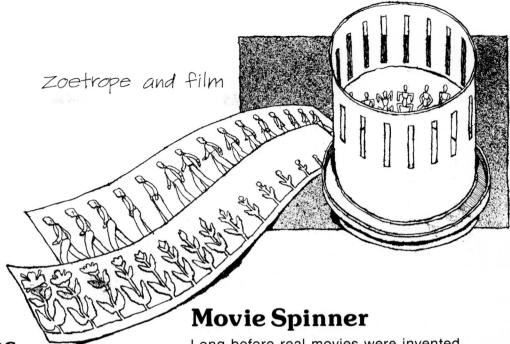

Zoetrope and film

Movie Spinner

Long before real movies were invented, people watched animated cartoons through a spinning viewer called a "zoetrope." It was a slotted cylinder lined with a sequence of action pictures, just like movie film. You spun the cylinder to animate the pictures, watching the show through the moving slots.

This old parlor game is quite simple to recreate with a cardboard cylinder (a 3-gallon ice cream carton is perfect), a Lazy Susan, and a strip of drawings.

Cut evenly spaced slots around the top of the carton, 1 inch down from the rim (see the sketch above). Paint the outside of the carton black.

Glue or tape it to the Lazy Susan.

For the cartoon "film" you need strips of paper about 5 inches wide and as long as the circumference of the cylinder. Wrap each strip around the slots, marking lightly with pencil between the slots. Pick activities that you can show in a sequence of drawings, such as a man exercising or a flower growing. Draw each picture where you made a pencil mark on the strip of paper. The pictures should change gradually, not suddenly, so the movie won't be jerky.

Wrap the strip in a circle, ends meeting, with the pictures on the *inside.*

Drop the strip inside the zoetrope so that it rests against the bottom. Spin the Lazy Susan and focus your eyes on the slots.

Tin Christmas Lanterns

In Mexico people often light their houses at Christmas with simple tin lanterns. They're decorated with lacy patterns of punched holes. Candlelight glowing through the holes creates dozens of flickering stars.

If you save up an assortment of tin cans and buy a few aluminum funnels, you can make Christmas lanterns for your family. The tin is easily pierced with a hammer and nail if you first freeze water in it.

Cans without ridges are the easiest to punch. Fill each one with water to ¼ inch below the rim. Leave the cans in the freezer for two days so the ice can get very hard.

Cut up paper bags to make patterns that will fit around the cans. Draw designs on the paper to follow as you punch the holes.

Lay the cans of frozen water on a towel (to soak up drips as the ice melts). Wrap the patterns around the cans and tape them down. Hammer evenly spaced nail holes through the lines of the pattern.

You don't have to try to freeze water in the funnels; they're sturdier. Just use a very sharp nail to punch a simple design. Leave the funnel tops on or ask a grownup to cut them off with tin snips.

In each punched can place a small candle and holder (votive candles in glass jars work well). Place the funnel, upside down, over top.

Gut Bucket

Have you ever seen an old folk instrument like this one-string bass? It has a nice, mellow sound when played either solo or in an ensemble. You can assemble the instrument with a metal bucket or wash tub, a broomstick, and a gut string.

Drill a hole in the bottom of the wash tub or bucket. Thread one end of the gut string through the hole and tie it on the inside to a washer. Cut slots in both ends of the broomstick. Fit the bottom slot on the rim of the overturned tub or bucket. Hold the broomstick upright and have someone tie the other end of the gut string to the top. The string should be stretched fairly tight.

To play the gut bucket, stand one foot on the bucket and pull on the broomstick to tighten the string so you can pluck a tune. The notes vary as you pluck up and down the string.

Foot racers are wobbly. Keeping your balance takes practice and teamwork.

Hawaiian Foot Racers

Shuffle along with your friends in these centipede sandals. See which team can make it across the lawn without toppling.

They're adapted from Japanese wooden clogs called *getas*. You make them longer and add extra thongs to carry two to five passengers.

The sketch on the left shows how to glue and nail small blocks of wood (2 inches square) to a 1 by 4-inch board to make the elongated clog. Allow 12 inches for each passenger. Drill ½-inch holes, as shown, to hold the thongs.

Cut six 30-inch strips of cotton cloth for each thong. Thread them through the toe hole of the wooden sole, knotting them underneath. Braid all six strips, divided into three pairs, for 1 inch. Then separate them, braiding three strips for each side strap. Poke the ends through the side holes and knot them underneath after fitting the thong to your foot.

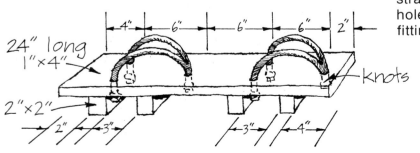

Walking Tall

Stilts put you way up in the air. Step up and look down. Suddenly, the ground is a lot farther away—and you are 4 feet taller.

They're easy to construct with a little help from your parents or a woodworking friend. It's worthwhile to make several pairs with foot rests set at different heights. This way, you and your friends can practice high stepping without having to wait for turns. Once you're good at it, you can have a giant walking race.

For the poles use 5 to 7-foot lengths of strong, straight-grained, 1 by 2-inch lumber. If 7 feet isn't tall enough or if you weigh more than 100 pounds, use 2 by 2-inch lumber.

Foot rests are cut from 4 by 6-inch blocks of 2 by 4-inch lumber. The simplest design is to cut a slanting piece off one long side of the block. (See the sketches below.)

Be sure to attach both foot rests at the same height on each pole or you'll walk with a limp. Glue the long side of the foot rest to the pole; secure it with four or five nails. Sand surfaces well; then varnish the wood to stop moisture from getting into the grain.

Have someone stand behind you, holding the tops of your stilts, until you get the feel of walking on them. Practice on a big, flat lawn.

Stiff-legged stilt walking is a curious experience. You shift your weight from side to side, using your hands to control your feet.

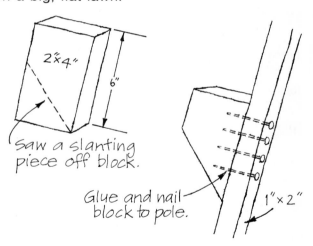

2"x4"

6"

Saw a slanting piece off block.

Glue and nail block to pole.

1"x 2"

Tin Can Walkers

For a simple version of stilts, use two 48-ounce juice cans and some rope.

Puncture the cans on two opposite sides, close to the top. Drink up the juice (or save what you can't drink in pitchers). Thread about 5 feet of rope through the holes of each can. Stand on the cans, holding the ends of the rope. Tie them at about waist height.

Trash Can Racers

These custom designed racers are in the same family as old-time soap box cars. The basic chassis is about the same, but the styling is updated.

Bright plastic trash cans replace wooden soap boxes for the main body parts. For trim and accessories, use small plastic housewares and junk—bowls for fenders, tumblers for blowpipes, ice cube trays for the radiator, and spray can lids for headlights.

Maybe you already have some of these things around the house. Even if you have to buy everything new, your racer should cost less than $30 to build.

Sketch your design on paper first. Then get your father or mother to help you build the chassis and turn your drawing into a car.

For the chassis you'll need these things:

- A 1 by 10-inch board, 5 feet long, to bridge axles.
- Two 2 by 3-inch boards, 3 feet long, for axles.
- Two 3-foot-long steel rods, ½ inch thick.
- Three feet of plumber's tape to attach rods to axles.
- A 4-inch ball-bearing Lazy Susan swivel, for steering.
- Four wagon wheels that fit the ½-inch rods.

Sketch 1 shows how the chassis goes together. It will be stronger if you screw it together rather than nail it.

First, make the axles by attaching the rods to the 2 by 3-inch boards with plumber's tape. Cut the plumber's tape into short lengths, bend it around the rods, and screw it into the boards. Join the axles to each end of the 1 by 10-inch board, fixing the Lazy Susan swivel between the front axle and the front end of the 1 by 10.

Following your design, arrange two or three sturdy plastic trash cans on the chassis. Cut them down where necessary—for example, if you want a curved bucket seat. A laundry basket strengthened with plywood makes a good truck bed.

Drill all the plastic parts at once. Attach them to the chassis with at least four screws and washers for each part. Use ¼-inch stove bolts with washers on both sides when you join two plastic parts; this will help prevent tearing the plastic.

After assembling the car, attach wheels to the axle rods and tie a long steering rope to the two ends of the front axle. For safety, add reflectors to the front and rear of the racer.

You can also add a pivoting brake that will drag on the ground when you pull the handle (see sketch 2). Use a 3-foot dowel or a 1 by 2-inch board, fixing it to the chassis with a 3-inch lag bolt.

Sketch 1

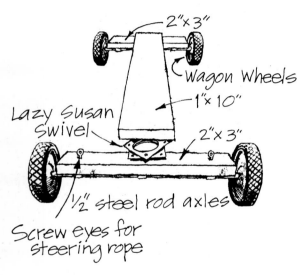

2"x 3"

Wagon Wheels

1"x 10"

Lazy Susan Swivel

2"x 3"

½" steel rod axles

Screw eyes for steering rope

Sketch 2

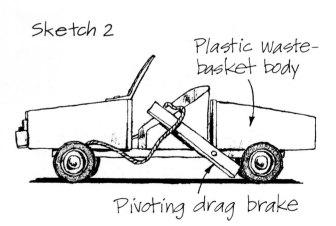

Plastic waste-basket body

Pivoting drag brake

Three trash can models lined up for a drag race display a variety of styling. Use your imagination and whatever plastic junk you can find to custom design your own car. Basic directions are on the opposite page.

A push from a friend starts her souped-up hot rod down a grassy slope.

Number 5 features a waste-basket lid windshield, ice cube tray radiator, and spray can lid headlights.

Mama Nature Crafts

If you are a hiker, explorer, camper, or beachcomber, you can have a lot of fun with this chapter. Even if you stick to your own back yard, you'll find wonderful materials to use in the following projects.

The world of Mama Nature is fascinating to observe. Keep your eyes open. Treasure the beauty and usefulness of leaves, feathers, rocks, twigs, seeds, pine cones, dry weeds, and berries. At the beach look for shells, driftwood, polished glass, and seaweed.

Some of the projects here are simple experiments—like growing crystals in a dish or rooting a carrot top in water. Some are old favorites—stringing flowers and building sand castles. Others will introduce you to crafts with an ancient tradition: basketry, ceramics, and woodcarving.

Kitchen Leftover Plants

Did you know you could raise a lacy, fernlike plant from a carrot top—or a fast-growing vine from a sweet potato? You can grow a whole garden from the seeds and cuttings of fruits and vegetables.

For your fernlike plant, cut 2 inches off the top of a carrot or a beet. (Cut off the leaves, too.) Set your beet or carrot—cut side down—in a dish with ½ inch of water in it. Change the water often. When roots appear, plant your carrot or beet top, cut side down, in a pot of moist sand. Set it in a sunny window and keep it wet.

To start a vine, stick three toothpicks in the sides of an old sweet potato. Set it in a glass of water with the toothpicks resting on the rim. The water should just cover the tip of the sweet potato. Put the glass in a place where the vine will get filtered sunlight. Pin up some strings so it can climb.

You can plant unpeeled garlic cloves, dry avocado pits, and citrus seeds in potting soil. Plant the garlic clove and avocado pit with the pointed ends up. Leave some of the avocado pit showing until it starts to grow—but cover up the clove. Soak the citrus seeds overnight before planting. Water these plants every few days, keep them in the sun, and watch nature take its course.

Sweet Potato

Carrot Top

Easter Grass

If you like to hunt eggs in tall grass, it might be fun to grow a miniature meadow right in your Easter basket. You can grow one in less than a week, using wheat seeds and a mineral substance called "vermiculite."

Both are available at some feed stores and nurseries. Check by phone first. You need about a pound of each for a large basket.

About a week before Easter, line the basket with plastic wrap and fill it with vermiculite, stopping 2 inches below the rim. Sprinkle the wheat seeds on top of the vermiculite. Set the basket in the sink and add water until the seed bed is moist. Don't water it again before Easter.

Set the basket in a pan in a place where the seed bed will get filtered sunlight. Cover the basket loosely with plastic wrap to keep it moist. After 2 days, remove the plastic. During the next few days, the wheat will begin to sprout—and by Easter morning you should have a lush nest for your eggs.

Natural Flea Collar

He's flea-free and handsome in a eucalyptus pod collar. It has a nice, tangy smell to people—but fleas hate it. In the spring, gather the bell-shaped pods around the roots of eucalyptus trees. Poke a needle threaded with dental floss through their soft centers. String enough so that you can slip the collar over your dog's neck; then tie the ends.

Sweet-smelling boot bouquet graces a garden wall. You can plant in all kinds of containers—not just in plain old clay pots. Look on the opposite page for a few ideas.

Flower Garland

In a garland of lavender blossoms, she's as pretty as May. The flowers are lilies of the Nile, their stems tied together with wire twists from bread wrappers.

A crookneck gourd holds plenty of popcorn for everyone. Look for other uses for gourds on the facing page.

Funny Planters

If you're a beginning gardener, planting in containers is a simple way to start. If you hunt around for some really unusual planters, your garden will be all the more interesting.

Geraniums and other bright flowers look cheery in an old boot, tennis shoe, or roller skate. The lace holes provide some drainage; poke a few more with a nail close to the sole. Put in a little gravel. Then fill the footwear with damp potting soil. Sow seeds, following the package directions, or plant with seedlings from the dime store.

Other decorative planters you might have on hand are toy trucks with big beds, an old baby bathtub, a felt or straw hat, or a fishbowl for a sweet potato vine. Directions for growing vines and other kitchen leftover plants are given on page 61. You might like to try some of them in your fancy planters.

Art from Gourds

These curious cousins of squash are easy to grow. Get a packet of mixed seeds and watch them develop during the summer into all kinds of smooth and bumpy shapes. You can't eat them—but you can make things with them after they dry out.

Plant the large, flat seeds in a sunny place where they will have something to climb up or down—like a trellis or a sloping bank.

Pick them when the skin feels fairly hard and the stem is getting dry. Hammer two nail holes near the stems so the gourds will dry faster. Rub them with floor wax to keep them from molding, and leave them in a cool, dry place for a few weeks.

By this time the seeds will be loose inside. They make a rattling sound when you shake them (this is why dry gourds are often used for maracas).

A cut crookneck gourd can be a shapely serving dish or a bird feeder. Just cut a wide circle out of one side and empty the seeds. Now you have a server.

If you want the gourd to be a bird feeder, thread string through the holes at the top of the neck and hang from a tree branch. Leave bird seed, bits of apple, and bread crumbs inside the cut-out hole.

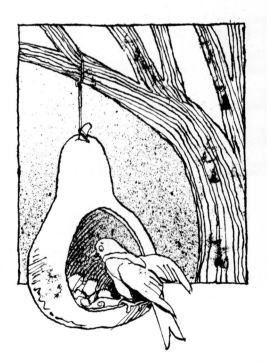

Leaf & Flower Notepaper

You can send a snippet from your garden to someone far away by sealing it to note paper with clear vinyl.

Collect flowers, leaves, and fine grasses that you can arrange in a pleasing bouquet. Dry them between newspapers under a stack of heavy books. This will take only 2 weeks or so if the plants are small.

Adhesive vinyl is sold by the yard at hardware stores. You can make note paper by folding plain paper in half.

Cut the vinyl (with its backing attached) a little bigger than the unfolded note paper. Remove the backing from half the vinyl and attach it to the back half of the note paper. Arrange the dried plants on the front. Hold them down and gradually peel off the rest of the backing. Smooth vinyl over the arrangement; then trim edges.

Whimmy Diddle

You've probably heard how two sticks rubbed together can start a fire. They can also set a propeller in motion. This is what happens when you operate a whimmy diddle.

You whittle this Appalachian folk toy from a green hardwood branch. You taper the body at one end and carve notches along its length. To its tip you nail a carved propeller blade.

When you rub a stick across the notches, you make the body vibrate. This causes the propeller blade to rotate. It changes direction as you change your strokes. If you rub the whimmy diddle briskly, the blade will spin very fast.

If you've never carved wood before, practice whittling for a while with a sharp jackknife. It's easiest to carve live wood, usually called green wood because it's young, light green, and sappy inside. Hold the knife with the blade pointing away from you. Carve off small slices at a time.

When you're ready to try a whimmy diddle, cut a 7 to 9-inch section of green hardwood branch for the body. Cut another 4 inches for the rubbing stick and 1½ inches for the propeller blade.

The sketches on the left show how to shape these three pieces. Whittle one end of the body and rubbing stick to taper them slightly. Carve six evenly spaced, V-shaped notches along the length of the body—about ⅛ inch deep. Carve the propeller blade so that its weight is concentrated equally at both ends.

Drill a hole through the center of the blade. Drive a 1-inch box nail through this hole and into the tip of the body. The blade should spin freely on this nail.

Try out the whimmy diddle. If the blade doesn't spin when you rub briskly, carve the body a little narrower and the notches a little deeper. Keep testing it; stop carving as soon as the propeller spins.

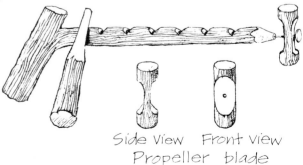

Side View   Front View
Propeller   blade

Depending on your taste, a crystal garden may or may not look beautiful. But it certainly does look weird. To grow the crystals, you spoon a special solution over bits of sponge, driftwood, cork, and other porous materials.

Crystal Garden

This strange, crystallized salt garden grows and changes daily. It's fascinating to watch. The result is almost indescribable. Maybe it resembles an eerie Martian landscape.

Grow the garden in a shallow glass pan or aluminum pie tin. Collect porous materials—such as tanbark, driftwood, lava rock, cork, and pieces of sponge. Arrange them in the container, piling them up to make a jumbled surface.

Mix up this solution: 4 tablespoons noniodized table salt, 4 tablespoons liquid bluing, 4 tablespoons water, and 1 tablespoon ammonia. Spoon it over the bits of porous material. Make sure the solution covers the bottom of the container. Drip just a little food coloring (one or two colors) over the garden.

Set the garden where you won't have to move it. Watch it change over the next four days. As the liquid travels to the surface, the water in it evaporates, leaving a saturated salt solution behind. Salts crystallize from this and keep growing until the solution dries out.

Sand Shapes

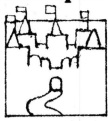

Sand is one of Mama Nature's marvels. Most of us like to sift it between our fingers and toes. And when it's wet, it's perfect for shaping, molding, and modeling. A sand shape won't last as long as other sculptures, and you can't take it home. But there's plenty more free sand on the beach so you can always make another one.

Mold sand by packing it firmly into a container—a coffee can or a deep bowl, for example. Flip the container over very fast. Tap its sides and carefully lift it off. The shape could be the first turret of a sand castle, a cake waiting for seaweed frosting, or whatever your imagination cooks up.

All kinds of gadgets come in handy for sculpting sand. A potato masher, fork, or spoon pressed into the damp surface makes nice impressions. A bricklayer's trowel, a table knife, or even a popsicle stick is useful for cutting corners and smoothing edges.

Keep a bucket of water by your side to keep the sand damp and workable.

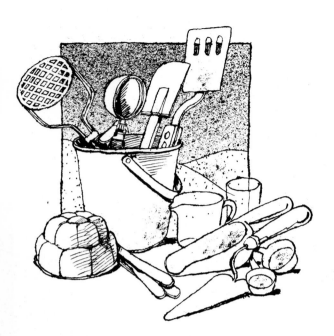

Molded Sand Candles

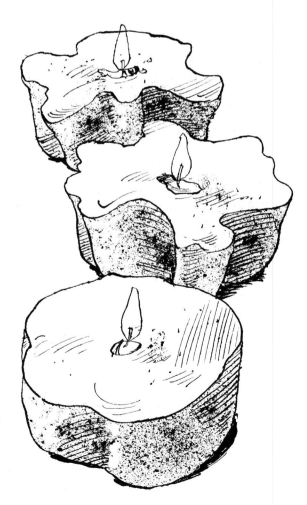

These would be fun to make the next time you spend a day at the beach.

Take along a camp stove, a large pan and enough water to half fill it, 1-pound coffee cans, paraffin wax (broken into pieces), crayons, oven mitts, and an old candle with a good wick.

Find a spot on the beach where the surf won't wash everything away before you're done. Boil the water on the camp stove. This will take a long time.

While waiting, you can dig and shape the mold. Dig a hole in damp sand about 4 inches deep. Mold it into an interesting shape. Stand the candle you brought along in the center of the mold so that its wick is level with the top.

Put enough pieces of paraffin wax in the 1-pound coffee cans so that they're about ⅔ full. Allow one can for each candle you plan to make. Add two or three crayons, for coloring, to each.

When the water boils, put on the oven mitts and carefully set the can of wax into the pan. **Be careful —*always* put can of wax in pan of water to melt; otherwise it might burst into flame.** Be sure to wear the oven mitts when you pour the melted wax into the mold.

Let the candle cool for about 2 hours. Then gently lift it out of the mold and brush off loose sand.

It won't be long before the surf fills the castle moat and washes away the towers. But while they stand, they're a fine example of sand architecture. And when the tide goes out again, you can always build another castle—maybe in a different style.

She's carving a sandy walrus. His drooping mustache is seaweed. His eyes and tusks are shells.

A popsicle stick comes in handy for shaping a castle tower. A tin can molds its shape. What other tools would be useful in sand sculpture?

Sand Cast Sculpture

To make a sand sculpture, you carve a mold in sand and pour in wet plaster of Paris. When it hardens you lift out a casting of whatever shape you carved.

Search the beach for treasures— feathers, rocks, shells, driftwood. Arrange them in the mold before you pour in the plaster of Paris.

Though you can make these castings at home in a sand box, they're especially fun to do at the beach. For each sculpture you'll need to take along 4 cups of plaster of Paris and 2 cups of fresh water. Also take a large coffee can for mixing the stuff and some kitchen tools for carving the sand.

Find a place on the beach that the tide won't reach. If the sand is dry, dampen it so it will be easier to mold. Scoop out a nice design. Driftwood, shells, rocks, and feathers can be arranged upside down in the mold. Later, they will be stuck to the surface of the plaster.

Dump the plaster of Paris into the water and let it stand about 2 minutes. Stir carefully for a couple of minutes, trying not to let air get in it. Wait 3 more minutes; then slowly and carefully pour the mixture into the sand mold.

The plaster will take about an hour to harden completely. After it begins to harden, dig away the sand from the plaster shape. Let it finish drying before you lift it out of the mold. If you want to hang the sculpture, push a hook into the surface just before the plaster sets.

Note: Plaster of Paris can set too quickly if you mix it too long or if you mix it with very warm water or salt water. If the water is extremely cold, the plaster may not set at all.

Clay Play

If you enjoyed making mud pies when you were little, you'll probably love ceramics. Ceramic clay is really a special kind of mud. You can dig it yourself out of creek beds and river banks. This is fun to do, but you must find a place that has real clay, not ordinary mud.

You can also buy ceramic clay at craft and art supply stores. It will last forever, but keep it moist and workable by storing it in an airtight plastic bag. If it does dry out, hammering it to bits and soaking it in water will restore it to a muddy consistency.

Protect your work table with oilcloth or plastic so the clay won't stick to it. Throw the lump of clay on the table a few times to help squeeze out air bubbles. Keep it very wet. Roll it, squeeze it, coil it, and push it into shape with your fingers and palms. If your sculpture is as big as your hand, scoop out the inside to make it hollow. Give its surface an interesting texture by printing it with odds and ends—spools, paper clips, coins, buttons, and kitchen utensils.

After you've sculpted something, let it harden for a few days. Then have it fired in a kiln if you want to keep it for a long time (air-dried pieces will last, too, but they break very easily). To find a nearby kiln, check with schools, recreation centers, and craft stores. Often these places will fire small pieces for a low price.

You can paint ceramics with water colors, acrylics, poster paints, or ceramic glazes. **Be careful—make sure the glazes are lead-free.** Fired clay has a nice warm color all on its own. If you glaze your piece, you'll have to fire it a second time, but the results can be very beautiful. See examples on the next page.

You can create interesting textures in clay by pressing small objects into the damp surface. Use rubber bands, buttons, paper clips, thread spools, and kitchen gadgets to work up a design.

Rock Molded Pots

This is a simple way to shape a ceramic pot. You just wrap a flat piece of clay around a smooth rock, which acts as a mold.

Part of the fun is finding just the right rocks. Search for them along river banks, lake shores, and beaches where water and weather have ground rocks smooth.

Roll out some clay between two ¼ or ½-inch boards to keep the slab an even thickness. Wrap the slab around the rock. Cut it with a table knife where the rock is widest. Flatten an area on the bottom of the pot so it will rest evenly on a table.

Loosen the clay from the rock without lifting it. Remove the clay when it's firm enough to hold its shape but not yet dry. Smooth the surface with a moistened finger. For firing the pot, read about clay above.

Simple, unfired red clay sculptures won't break as long as you handle them with care. The owl's head is the folded edge of a rolled-out slab. Slip a piece of yarn under the fold to hang him up. Form feathers by pinching the clay. The face is also shaped by folding; the features were cut out with a table knife. For details, see page 69.

Winnie the Pooh and his friends gather in the forest for a honey pot picnic. These storybook figures were modeled from clay, bisque-fired, and then painted with water colors. For more details about work-ing with clay, see page 69.

These delicate ceramic pieces were formed with care and atten-tion to detail. Tiny animals crawl in and out of the unglazed cup. Like the rosebuds on the jug, they were glued in place with a mixture of clay and water called "slip." For more details about clay, see page 69.

Leaf Print Tiles

The design on the face of these tiles is a tracing of leaves. You press them into a flat slab of clay with a rolling pin.

You need some low-fire red clay and a sheet of acetate from an art supply store. To protect your work table and also to prevent the clay from sticking, lay down a yard of oilcloth, wrong side up. Find two 18-inch strips of wood about ½ inch thick. As you roll out the clay, these strips will keep the edges straight and guide the thickness of the slab.

Gather a variety of leaves with interesting shapes and vein patterns. Geranium leaves, ferns, and reedy grasses leave fine impressions in clay.

Take four or five handfuls of moist clay and throw the lump down on the oilcloth several times. This helps squeeze out air bubbles.

Lay the strips of wood about 8 inches apart on either side of the clay lump. Roll the lump into a flat slab with a rolling pin.

Arrange the leaves and grasses on the slab, leaving plenty of room for a border around each tile. Lay the sheet of acetate over them. Run the rolling pin over the leaves to press them into the clay.

Using a ruler for a straightedge, cut out the tiles with a table knife. Carefully lift them with a spatula and dry them on cardboard covered with aluminum foil. Pick off the leaves as they dry and curl up.

After about a week, the tiles will be ready to fire in a kiln. Find one by looking in the Yellow Pages under "Ceramics" for a craft store or check with a school or recreation center near you.

Have them fired twice. The first, called a "bisque" firing, hardens them enough so they won't break easily. At this point you can paint them with glaze if you want to and then have them glaze-fired.

Use the glaze to outline the leaf shapes or to paint a border around the edge of the tiles. To keep the border straight, hold a strip of cardboard on the clay and brush the glaze away from it.

After laying a sheet of acetate over the leaves, press them into the clay with a rolling pin. Cut tiles out with a table knife. Use a ruler to keep edges straight.

Basket Weaving

Basketry is fun to do outdoors on a hot summer's day because you work with soaking wet reeds. This ancient craft is really very simple once you learn one weaving technique.

You weave on a framework of reeds called "spokes." At first they are arranged just like bike wheel spokes. As you form the sides of the basket, you pull the spokes upright. The reeds you weave with are called "weavers."

Rattan reeds (from rattan palms) come in two shapes—flat and round—and several sizes. They are sold in 1-pound bundles at some craft and hobby stores. Since the same reeds are used to make chair seats, check with a chair caning shop if the hobby store doesn't supply them. You can make at least three baskets from two bundles.

Thick, round reeds are best for spokes. For variety you might want to use two kinds of weavers—flat reeds and narrow, round ones.

Soften the reeds so they will bend easily by soaking them in water for 15 minutes to 1 hour (the time depends on how thick and how dry they are). As you weave your basket, keep dipping it in water when it starts to dry out.

Decide how big a basket you want to weave before cutting the spokes. The bigger the basket, the more spokes you'll need. For all sizes, cut an even number of long spokes—all the same length—plus one that is half as long as the others. Each long spoke must reach across the basket's base and travel all the way up both sides.

To start with, you might want to weave the small basket holding spools of thread, shown in the photo on the left. This one is 3 inches tall and 4 inches wide. To make it you will need two bundles of round reeds—No. 5 size for spokes and No. 2 for weavers. Cut four long spokes, 18 inches each. Make the short spoke 9 inches long.

Bind the spokes together with the first weaver as shown in photo 1 (right). Then spread them out evenly—like sun's rays—and start weaving. Stop when only ½ inch of the weaver is left. Use a knitting needle to open a space along the nearest spoke so you can push in the end of the weaver. Put a new one in the opposite side of the same spoke.

When the base is as wide as you want it, pull the weaver tight. This will pull the spokes upright to form the basket shape. If the base feels wobbly, you can add more spokes at this point. Slide new ones between the weavers on each side of the first spokes.

As you weave the sides, press the center of the base up in a dome shape. Try to keep the spokes evenly spaced and the woven rows perpendicular to the spokes.

When you have woven close to the top of the basket, cut the spoke ends so they are 3 inches long. Form a border by weaving one spoke over and under the next ones or looping it back into basket sides as shown in photos 5 and 6 below.

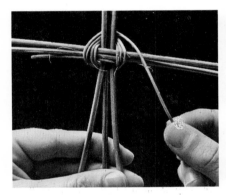

1) Cross the centers of four long spokes. Push the short spoke through the center. Lash them all together with the first weaver.

2) Spread the spokes. Start weaving with the rest of the first weaver, going over the first spoke, under the next—until only ½ inch is left.

3) At the end of the first weaver, use a knitting needle to open a space along the nearest spoke. Insert the weaver end. Put a new one into the opposite side of the same spoke.

4) To begin or end a flat weaver, overlap ends, as shown above.

5) To loop a border, poke the 3-inch spoke ends back into the basket beside the next spoke.

6) To weave a border, pass one spoke end over and under the next and pull tight.

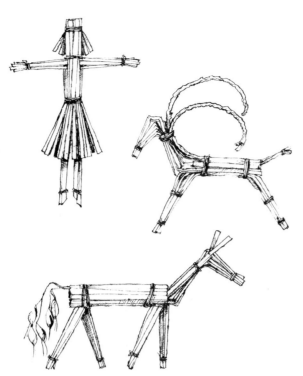

Bundled Straw Figures

Simple animals, figures, and stars of bundled straw make handsome decorations for the Christmas tree. Gather the straw yourself from a field or ask for loose pieces at a stable or feed store. Pick through it for thick, sturdy tubes; flattened and broken straw doesn't work very well.

To soften the straw so you can bend it easily, soak it in warm water. Put something heavy on it to keep it submerged. Let it drain a few minutes. Then cut it into several different lengths from 4 to 10 inches.

Make a star by tying straws together with bright crochet thread.

Start forming an animal or a figure from a bundle of eight 10-inch tubes. Bend back two straws for a head, tying at the neck. Divide straws from the bundle for legs and tail—or form them from separate bundles and tie them to the body.

Save seed husks for bushy tails, hair, and decorations.

Knock out a tune on the bamboo chimes with a dowel. The shorter the chime, the higher it will sound.

Bamboo Xylophone

Bamboo spreads very quickly and often needs to be cut back. You can use the cut-off shoots to make an upright xylophone.

Bamboo poles consist of short, hollow sections separated by solid rings. The solid places are slightly wider. To make the xylophone chimes, cut the sections apart with a small handsaw. You end up with short pieces that are open at one end, blocked at the other.

The first chime will be a full section. It will produce the lowest note. Cut the others in graduated lengths—like a staircase. The last and shortest chime will make the highest note.

For the xylophone's base, you need an 18-inch-long board and eight 4-inch nails. Spacing the nails evenly, hammer them right through the board so the points stand up like spikes on the other side. Fix the chimes, in order, on the spikes by pressing the solid bottom of each one over the nail and twisting it in place (see the sketches below).

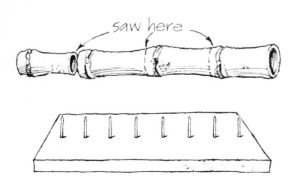

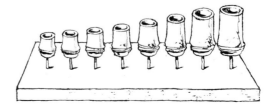

Miniature Landscape

With a few garden ingredients, you can create a miniature world for your cars, trucks, and dolls. Houses are bricks with shingle roof tops. A line of twigs makes a pole fence. Plant cuttings stuck in the ground create lush foliage. Dribbled pebbles provide a path.

Nature Puppets

The makings of these nature puppets were gathered during a walk in the woods. Features are seeds, pods, acorns, and leaves. They're fixed in place with a little white glue and bits of clay. Heads are glued to branches and dowels. Decorate with imagination!

Kitchen Capers

Here's a chance to play with your food. In this chapter your table manners can be as messy as you please. These projects are for food lovers—people who love to eat; people who enjoy the colors, shapes, smells, and textures of food.

Some of these foods taste so delicious you'll do plenty of nibbling as you work with them. One thing's certain: most projects won't last very long after you make them.

Your kitchen cupboards will probably supply you with most of what you'll need. Check with your mother before you start rummaging or you may accidentally upset her dinner plans.

Fruit & Nut Figures

Prune and apricot characters like Mr. Boxer (on the right) would make delicious Christmas gifts. You string dried fruit on wire threaded through a wood base.

For each figure, hammer two nail holes all the way through a small block of wood. Cut two 9-inch lengths of narrow rustproof wire (such as 16 gauge) for the legs and body. Cut a 5-inch length for arms. Thread the longer pieces through the holes in the block, leaving ½-inch ends extending underneath.

Hammer these ends flat and cover them with masking tape. Also cover the other ends of the wires with tape so you won't cut yourself.

String dried apricots, apples, prunes, figs, and dates on the wires to form the legs and body. When you reach the shoulders, thread the 5-inch length of wire through the two body wires. Add more fruit for the arms.

Decorate a walnut head with paint or flow pens. When it's dry, hammer a nail hole where its neck should be. Do the same to two more walnuts—for hands. Poke the ends of the wires through these holes.

They're stringing delicious fruit and nut characters to give away for Christmas.

Noodle Art

Noodles come in a wide variety of shapes and sizes. Many have interesting Italian names like rigatoni, manicotti, tagliarini and, of course, macaroni and spaghetti.

Some are named for what they look like—bow ties, wagon wheels, and shell macaroni.

You can glue different shapes together to form lacy ornaments for the Christmas tree. Gather an assortment—from the grocery store and Italian delicatessens—for a Christmas glue-in.

Use white glue and work on wax paper. The paper will peel off the ornament after it dries. Dab the glue on the noodles with a toothpick or a small brush.

When you join two curved pieces, add smaller pieces for bracing. The snowflakes (on the left) are strengthened with ditali (tiny pasta rings) and elbow macaroni.

The ornaments take about 2 hours to dry. They break easily, but if you handle them gently they will last for several seasons. And they're fun to repair.

Eggshell Mosaic

Smash, crash, crackle! One way to deal with the remains of Easter is to break them up for a mosaic. Draw a simple picture with plenty of white space. Fill it in with glued-down bits of colored eggshells.

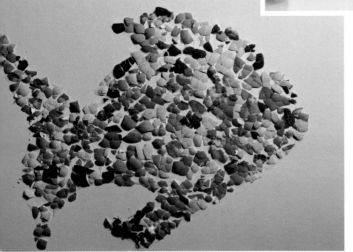

Collection of Easter art includes dip-dyed eggs, waxed eggs, fabric, yarn, and sequin eggs, seed eggs, and tissue collage eggs. These and other ways to decorate are described on the facing page.

Easter Egg Art

For your next Easter egg hunt, why not hide some surprises? You can try many different ways to make many pretty eggs. A few are suggested below, and you'll come up with new ideas as you start to experiment.

If your decoration is going to turn into a special work of art, it makes sense to blow the egg first. Then you can keep it for a long time.

To blow an egg, poke a small hole in one end with a needle. Push the needle deep inside to break the yoke. Then poke a slightly bigger hole in the other end. Holding the egg over a bowl, blow through the smaller hole until the shell is empty. Save the raw egg for breakfast or cupcakes. Rinse the shell well and let it dry.

Egg Faces

With flow pens, draw bright, funny, happy, sad, and mad faces on blown eggs. To keep them from smearing, spray them with fixative from an art supply store (get help from a grownup). Glue on yarn hair, eyebrows, beards, and mustaches.

Paper Collage Eggs

Glue torn or cut tissue paper to blown eggs with white glue or liquid starch. Or make a collage with small pictures and words cut out of a magazine.

Fabric Eggs

Cut out a 6-inch circle and gather its edge to make a bag for an egg. Stitch ribbon to the bag to cover the opening. Turn another egg into patchwork by gluing on tiny squares of fabric.

Striped Eggs

Paint an egg with white glue and wrap it with rows of colorful yarn. Push the rows together with a toothpick.

Dip & Dye Eggs

Stick a pattern of masking tape on a plain egg. Press it securely in place. Dip it in a dark vegetable coloring, Easter egg dye, or crepe paper soaked in hot water. After it dries, remove the tape. Leave the masked areas white or dip the egg again in a lighter color.

Waxed Eggs

Draw a heavy crayon pattern on an egg. Dip it in a dark color. Melt the crayon marks by putting the egg in a 200° oven for a few minutes and wiping with paper towel. Dip in a lighter color. This second color will fill in the pattern you drew with the crayon.

Seed Eggs

Roll eggs first in white glue and then in split peas, poppy seeds, fennel, barley, sunflower seeds—or any other seeds you can think of. The result? Elegant eggs.

Potato Prints

Potatoes may be the world's most popular vegetable for printing. You can stamp them on paper again and again, and they don't wear out. And they're easy to carve.

If you're not used to working with a sharp knife, you can also make a design on half a potato with a cookie cutter. Press its sharp edge into the potato and trim around the shape so it will stand out.

A messy but fun way to print with potato halves is to make ink pads with sponges. (You could also use several layers of paper towels.) Soak the pad with plenty of poster paint. Stamp the cut side of the potato on the wet pad and then again on paper.

Can you recognize which fruits and vegetables they used to make these prints?

Fruit & Vegetable Designs

Cut a red cabbage in half and notice the beautiful ripples formed by its leaves. Many other fruits and vegetables have interesting patterns of skin, pulp, and seeds hidden inside them, too.

You can capture these designs on paper. Just roll water-based printing ink on the cut side of the fruit or vegetable. Then press it on a sheet of paper over several layers of newspaper. Use the printed paper for gift wraps or note cards. Combine different shapes to make a fruit and vegetable picture to hang on the wall.

Besides cabbage, you might try halves of onions, artichokes, oranges, apples, mushrooms, green peppers, and string beans. Let them drain, cut side down, for a while before you print with them.

If you don't have any ink on hand, poster paint works almost as well. Pour a little of either on the bottom of a glass baking dish or cookie sheet. Roll it out with a brayer (a roller on a stick; buy one at an art supply store). Use the brayer to coat the cut side of the fruit or vegetable. You should be able to print several times with one coating.

If you don't have a brayer, try pouring poster paint on several layers of paper towels and stamping the fruit or vegetable in it.

After drawing on the paraffin with a flow pen, carve the design with a linoleum cutting tool or a jack-knife.

Paraffin Block Cards

You can turn out a stack of Christmas cards very quickly by printing them on a paraffin block. Paraffin is as smooth and soft as butter to carve. If you make a mistake you can either turn the block over and start again or, with an adult's help, melt the paraffin and pour it into a square mold to form a new block.

Paraffin blocks are sold inexpensively at grocery stores. One package contains four blocks, 2½ by 5 inches large. Buy blank cards at a stationery or art supply store or make your own from folded paper. You will also need water-based printing ink and a brayer to roll it.

To smooth the surface of the block, cover it with aluminum foil and iron it lightly with a warm iron. Draw your design with a flow pen. Carve it with the small blade of a jackknife or a linoleum cutting tool. If you make letters, be sure to draw them backwards.

Brush off loose pieces of paraffin. Rub the block with the back of a spoon to smooth down any ridges left from cutting.

Squeeze the ink onto a cookie sheet or glass baking dish. Roll it out with the brayer; then roll it on the block. Press your card over the block and rub it with the back of a spoon. Lift off your print.

If ink builds up in the carved-out areas as you print more cards, rinse the block, dry it, and apply more ink.

Roll water-based printing ink evenly over the block.

Press a blank card over the block and rub the surface with the back of a spoon. Then lift off your print.

Dried Apple Dolls

Apple head dolls look very much like grandmas and grandpas with plenty of wrinkles. But you can turn a dried apple into any sort of crusty character. Each face will be individual, because no two apples shrivel up exactly the same way.

Dry three or four large red apples at one time. Washington Delicious work very well, especially if they've been stored for awhile. The apples should be pulpy and not too juicy.

Peel them, leaving a little skin at the top and the bottom. Scoop out two eye hollows on each apple with a spoon. This will leave a raised bump for a nose. Rub the apples well with halves of lemon.

To hang the apples up to dry, you need 9 inches of rustproof wire for each head. Poke the wire through the bottom of the core. Push it through the top and bend its end into a hook. Form the bottom end of the wire into a loop.

Hang the apples for about 3 weeks away from sunshine and drafts. On the second day, spray them with disinfectant.

When the apples are dry, cut slits for the eyes and mouth with fingernail scissors. Thread white beads on a pin, dip them in white glue, and push them into the mouths for teeth. Small pebbles would do just as well.

Dab glue on dark beads or buttons, pushing them into the slits you cut for eyes. Paint rosy cheeks with water colors. After everything dries, brush the faces with glossy acrylic polymer (from an art supply store) to give them a healthy glow.

For the bodies you'll need empty dish detergent bottles. Fill them with sand to keep them steady. Poke arm holes in the sides with a nail. Thread pipecleaner arms through the holes. Push the wire necks of the apple heads inside the bottles until the heads rest on the bottle openings. Glue the heads in place with white glue.

To complete the dolls, glue on hair of cotton wool or yarn. Wrap the bodies in fabric scraps, stitched together or glued to the bottles.

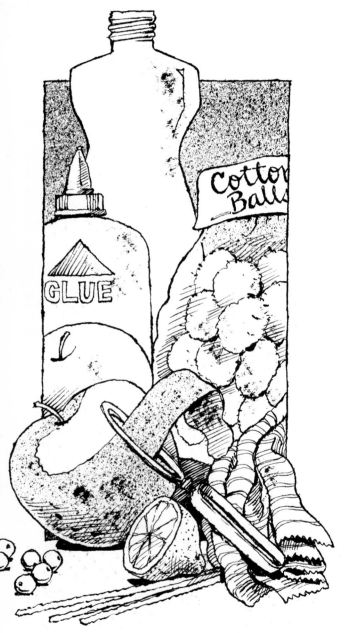

Food Creatures

Use your imagination to piece together a menagerie from fruits and vegetables. The serpent shown here is strung together with a needle and button thread. A dried fruit roll tongue darts out of his lemon head. The sheep's wool is cauliflower. The rabbit is a squash. Features are fixed in place with toothpicks and pins—they can be removed later if you want your creature to join a salad or stew.

Fish Print

Make a rubbing of your catch before you cook it. If you use water-based paints or ink, you can wash the fish off afterward.

Catch or buy a medium-size fish with fairly big scales and fins. This one is a sole. Brush it with one or several colors. Lay rice paper or tissue paper over it and carefully smooth it down to cover the fish completely. Gently rub the scales and fins. Then lift off the print. One painted fish should yield four or five prints.

Pucker-faced grannies owe their beauty to dried apples. You'll be surprised how easy it is to make these realistic dolls. Directions are given on the opposite page.

Rolling Nuts

Watch these creatures skitter along on marbles. Their bodies are halves of walnut shells. You cut heads, tails, and features from felt scraps or paper and glue them to the shells.

After the glue dries, set the shells on marbles and let your creatures roll down a sloping board.

Pumpkin Sculpture

Fat Halloween pumpkins in need of faces usually get carved into jack-o-lanterns. But for variety, you might like to try a new kind of face—like the pumpkin sculpture on the right.

Pick out a big pumpkin that looks good for carving a funny or scary face. If it has a few bumps that will do for a nose, chin, or warts, part of your job is already done.

With a vegetable peeler, remove the skin from half the pumpkin. Draw large features on the face with a pencil or nail.

Check the thickness of the pumpkin by cutting a wedge out of the back. This tells you how deep you can carve before you reach the hollow inside. Put the wedge back in the pumpkin.

Carve down and away from the lines you drew, using a paring knife or a jackknife. When you're finished, paint the features with poster paint to make them show up better.

Enjoy your pumpkin friend while he lasts—if he's kept outside he may be around for a week or more.

Wrapped Honeycomb Candles

These candles are easy to make and quite safe because you don't need to melt the wax. All you do is roll a sheet of beeswax around a wick.

Many craft and hobby stores stock both the beeswax and wicking. Check by phone first. Ask for metal core wicking.

The beeswax sheets come in a variety of colors. You can cut them easily with scissors. You join two sheets by pressing them together; their honeycomb surfaces interlock.

Two sheets will roll into a fatter cylinder. If you roll up the long side of a sheet, you'll get a tall, narrow candle; rolling up the short side will produce a shorter one.

Cut the wick a little longer than the side you want to roll up. Lay it close to the edge of the sheet. Fold the edge over the wick and press it down to hold the wick in place. Then roll up the candle.

Cut out decorations from different colors of beeswax. Press them into the honeycomb sides of the candle.

Popcorn Puppets

Puffy popcorn people make grand old-fashioned ornaments to dance in the Christmas tree. Of course, popcorn tastes good at any time of year, so you might want to string these puppets just for fun on a summer afternoon.

Pop a huge bowlful so you have plenty to eat as you string. Let the popcorn sit for a day or two to soften; it will be less likely to break. It's best not to butter it, but salt won't hurt.

String it on thin wire such as 26 gauge (the higher the gauge number, the thinner the wire). Cut lengths of 6 or 8 inches for arms and legs and about 10 inches for body and head.

Work carefully to avoid pricking your fingers—the cut ends of the wire are sharp. Poke the wire through a soft part of each kernel close to the middle.

When the body wire is full, bend one end into a loop for a head. Twist the end of the wire around the neck. Arms and legs are single strands, bent in the middle. Twist the arms around the neck. Bend the bottom end of the body wire around the center of the leg strand. Gently bend the arms and legs in a lively dancing position.

Here are a few things you can make with baker's clay. They look good to eat, but watch out—they taste terrible, and they're hard as rocks. Look for recipe and details on making puppet, train, and jewelry on the opposite page.

Two furry friends enjoy a dolls' tea party in the garden. The menu is chocolate cake, apples, and oranges modeled from melted crayons. Directions for these and other doll-sized tidbits appear on the facing page.

Baker's Clay

This terrible-tasting dough is wonderful for sculpture. You shape it and bake it. The result is a very hard, permanent cookie—but you wouldn't want to eat it.

To make the dough, mix 1 cup of flour to 1 cup of salt. Add just a little water until the dough feels like modeling clay—not too dry, not too sticky. You can color small amounts of the dough with food coloring—or wait and paint the finished cookies with poster paints.

Shape the dough just as if it were clay. Start with a rolled-out slab; then cut the slab into pieces you can model with your fingers. Experiment with kitchen utensils to mark designs or to cut out shapes.

The puppet, train, and necklaces shown on the opposite page are made of several cookies baked separately and strung together afterwards. Before baking, poke holes in the dough so you can link the parts together. Push matchstick axles through the cars before you bake them. Glue on wheels afterwards.

Bake the cookies in a 200° oven until they're very hard. Check them after 5 minutes. The baking time depends on the size of the cookies. A very big one may take a whole hour.

Crayon Doll Food

Serve these shiny wax snacks to your dolls for lunch. They are modeled from melted crayons and candle stubs. You wait until the wax is cool enough to handle but still soft. Then you shape it with buttered fingers.

Unless you've made candles before, have a grownup help you melt the wax. It gets very hot. **Be careful—*always* put can of wax in a pan of water to melt; otherwise it may burst into flame.**

Gather together some tin cans (one for each color), oven mitts, a wide pan, and a few candle stubs and crayons. Line a cookie sheet with wax paper to hold the cooling crayons. Keep more wax paper on hand for later batches of crayon food.

Put a few crayons and candle stubs in each can. You need only a small pool of melted wax for each food item. Boil a few inches of water in the pan. Set the cans in the water until the wax is melted. With your oven mitts on, take out the cans. Pour small pools of two or three colors on the wax paper.

Take off your oven mitts and rub plenty of margarine on your fingers. Wait 2 or 3 minutes for the wax to cool and form a hard skin. Then peel it off and model it into a simple fruit, vegetable, cookie, or cake shape. If it hardens faster than you can shape it, hold it briefly under warm water to make it soft again.

Whimsy Bread

Squeeze it, roll it, punch it, poke it . . . . No matter how roughly you treat this sculpture, it will still taste delicious with butter and honey. You model it out of soft, stretchy bread dough. The longer you work on it, the better it tastes.

If someone in your family knows how and can help you, mix up a batch of white yeast bread dough. Follow the recipe to the point of shaping the loaves. You can also use frozen bread dough from the grocery store.

To get the dough ready for sculpture, you have to knead it for awhile. If you're using frozen dough, first be sure it's completely thawed.

Kneading is lots of fun to do. First you sprinkle a bread board or wooden table top with a little flour. Rub plenty on your hands, too.

With your palms, press the dough flat on the floured board. Fold it toward you, giving it another push. Keep flattening it and folding it, turning the ball of dough from time to time. Try to knead rhythmically (singing or listening to music helps).

When the dough is smooth and satiny, it will be ready for sculpture.

Roll it into a flat cake with a rolling pin. Think up a good loaf shape—something that will surprise everyone in the family.

She rolls the kneaded dough into a flat cake, ready for sculpture.

Following the outline of a bowl, she cuts strips of dough to twist into sun rays.

After rising and baking, the dough will get much fatter. So make your shape skinnier than you want it to be in the end.

Form arms and legs by rolling pieces of dough between your palms. You can also twist them (like the sun rays in the photo on the right) or braid them.

Join parts of your sculpture by pinching the dough together. Leave at least 2 inches of space between parts you want to stay separated—like legs—or they may grow together when the dough rises. To attach small shapes (like eyes, nose, and smile), poke a hole in the big lump of dough and set the small dough shape in the hole.

When you're finished modeling, set your sculpture on a greased cookie sheet. Cover it with a damp cloth and let it rise in a warm place. Usually the inside of a switched-off oven has just the right temperature. After about 45 minutes, the sculpture will be fat and puffy.

Mix an egg with a tablespoon of water. Brush this over the sculpture to give it a shiny, golden crust. Bake it in a 350° oven for about half an hour (until the crust is browned). Cool it on a wire rack.

Use your fanciful sculpture to liven up the next family meal.

To add features, poke a hole and drop in a small lump of dough.

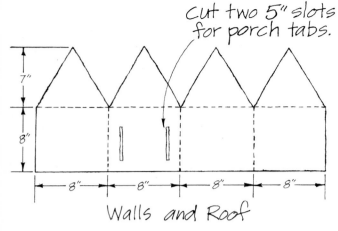

Cut two 5" slots for porch tabs.

Walls and Roof

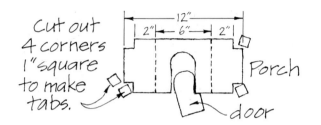

Cut out 4 corners 1" square to make tabs.

Porch

door

Sugar Plum House

Lots of sweet nibbling goes into the construction of this house. It makes a festive centerpiece at Christmas or any time of the year, and everyone will want to taste one of its peppermint roof tiles or chocolate shingles.

For decoration, you need about 3 pounds of assorted candies. If you *really* have a sweet tooth, you may need even more.

Transfer the patterns (on the left) to heavy paper. Trace them on cardboard and cut out the house and porch. Fold along the dotted lines. Tape the house sides and roof together with masking tape. Insert the porch tabs through the slots in the front of the house.

Make frosting from a packaged mix or by using the following recipe: beat 2 egg whites until stiff; add ½ teaspoon cream of tartar and 1 pound confectioner's sugar; beat until the frosting is fairly stiff.

Spread the frosting on the cardboard house with a rubber spatula, working as fast as you can.

Decorate the house by pressing candies into the frosting.

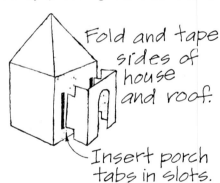

Fold and tape sides of house and roof.

Insert porch tabs in slots.

Alphabet Cookies

These cookies spell delicious, crumbly words. The letters are shaped from a special vanilla dough that handles like modeling clay. It might be fun to make a batch of them with your friends at your next birthday party. Make enough letters so everyone can spell his or her name.

To make the dough, measure 4½ cups unsifted all-purpose flour into a bowl. Add 1½ cups butter, cut into small pieces. Mix with your fingers until the flour and butter form fine crumbs. Mash 3 hard-cooked egg yolks with ¾ cup sugar and stir into the flour mixture. Blend 3 raw egg yolks with 1½ teaspoons vanilla, and stir into the flour mixture with a fork.

Press the mixture with your hands into a firm ball. Keep the ball covered. Work with the dough at room temperature but refrigerate it if you make it ahead.

Roll out the dough. Cut 3 or 4-inch strips that you can roll between your palms to make ropes. Shape the ropes into letters. Flatten them slightly so they're about ¼ inch thick. If you like, decorate the letters with colored sugar or chocolate. Bake 25 to 30 minutes in a 300° oven.

Hansel and Gretel's dream house is studded with peppermints, jelly beans, licorice twists, and lollipops. Make your own dream house for sweet snacking. See directions on the opposite page.

Joe will have no trouble finding his place at the birthday table. Delicious alphabet cookies spell it out for him. They're easy to shape, using the cookie dough recipe on the facing page.

Rainy Day Dreams

Sometimes it seems as if there's nothing to do. Maybe it's raining outside. Maybe you've been watching too much TV—or maybe it's a slow afternoon for no special reason at all.

To brighten your spirits at times like these, it helps to have something quick, easy, and fun to do. Here are a few such spare-time filler-uppers. They're all easy to make, do, and enjoy. These mini-projects won't turn out to be your finest works of art. They're just simple pleasures—things like blowing soap bubbles and blasting off a balloon rocket. Hopefully, they'll give you a few giggles the next time you're stuck with a rainy day.

But don't wait for it to rain—try one of these spur-of-the-moment projects right now.

Fingertip Puppets

Most puppets fit over your fingers. So why not make them right on your fingertips? Just draw tiny faces on your fingers with flow pens. Attach hats (bottle caps, thimbles, cotton balls, or paper) with masking tape rolled into circles, sticky side out. Think up a play with 10 characters.

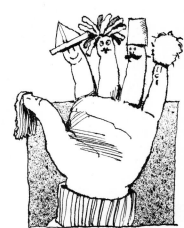

Metal Music

To everyone else, this may sound like a fork banging on the bars of an oven rack. That's actually what's going on. But to you it will sound like a strange metallic melody. The music, carried on a string, is for your ears alone.

Weave a 36-inch length of string over and under the bars of an oven rack. Hold both ends to your ears. Have someone strike up a tune with a fork or a spoon.

Button Whirl

To make this simple spinning toy, you need about 4 feet of string and a large button with two holes. Pass the string through both holes and tie the ends so that the button is threaded on a long loop. Whirl the loop of string like a jump rope until it's tightly wound up. Then pull on the ends. The button spins and dances as the string unwinds.

If you get the string very tightly wound, the button will hum as it spins.

Balloon Rocket

This rocket blasts off when you let go of an inflated balloon. Besides the balloon, you need a long piece of string, a drinking straw, and some tape.

Tie one end of the string to a high place in your room, like a curtain rod. This is the moon, or Mars—or wherever your rocket is headed. Thread the string through the drinking straw.

Blow up the balloon. Have somebody tape it to the straw. With one hand, hold the blown-up balloon. With your other hand, hold the string so that it's stretched tight. Now let go of the balloon. As the air escapes from it, your rocket races up the string.

Tambourine

You can make plenty of noise with two aluminum pie pans and a handful of beans. Staple the rims together, spacing the staples close enough so the beans won't leak out. Glue on some trimming.

Paper Clip Necklace

Among many things you can do with paper clips is to link them together to make a necklace. This jangly chain combines standard metal paper clips with bright plastic ones.

Face Fuzz

A hairy disguise can turn you into a wild man of the woods. He used curtain fringe for heavy brows, cotton wool for a beard, and knotted yarn for a mustache—all attached with adhesive tape.

Lunch Bag Puppet

This cat is nothing more than a decorated paper bag. Fold the bottom of the bag flat against one side. Slip your fingers inside the fold. Open and close it to make the puppet talk.

Wheel Dressing

Dress up your bike with crepe paper. Weave streamers in and out of the spokes. When you ride, the wheels will flash swirls of color.

Magazine Cut-ups

Treasure old magazines. They're full of collage possibilities. Search for pictures of faces. Cut out as many eyes, noses, mouths, ears, and heads of hair as you can find. Mix them up, rearrange them, and paste funny faces on a piece of paper. Look for words to cut out and paste to make sentences. Send a magazine letter to a friend.

Soap Sculpture

Soap is easy to carve. Even a table knife will chip it away, although a jackknife works faster. With a nail, draw something like a simple animal or a boat on one side of the soap cake. Carve away from the lines you drew. Polish the cut edges by wetting the soap and smoothing the edges with your fingers.

Flower Color

Tint a white flower to match your bedspread or your rug. As you do it, you'll see for yourself the way plants drink water through their stalks—and where the water goes.

Fill glasses halfway with water and enough food coloring to tint the water a bright color. Add a white carnation or a white daisy. Watch the flower turn green, yellow, red, or blue over the next few hours.

Invisible Ink

You can write a secret message to a friend by using a small paint brush and lemon juice instead of ink. The letters won't show up until your friend presses them with a warm iron.

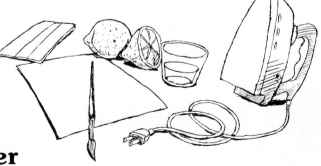

Bubbler

Blow gently through this simple pipe and fill the air with floating bubbles.

Poke a pencil hole 1 inch from the bottom of a paper cup. Stick a drinking straw through the hole halfway into the cup. Pour enough dish detergent into the cup to cover the straw, adding a little water and a few drops of food coloring. Blow until bubbles froth over the rim of the cup and float away.

Index

Designers

Laverne Atkins and Sandra Sanders (puppets, page 75). Laurie Capparell (masks, page 23). Bob Gebhart (flip card, page 8; castle, page 23; raft, page 52; zoetrope, page 55; xylophone, page 74). Suki Graef (bean bags, page 41; candy house and cookies, page 90). Jean Heighton (apple dolls, page 82). Francoise Kirkman (sock dolls, page 39; ragbraid bag, page 43). Whitney Lane (food creatures, page 83). Rick Morrall (racers, page 58). Pat Scarlett (kites, page 10; eraser prints, page 17). Roz Wagner (hardware art, page 49). Susan Warton (bean bags and puppets, page 32; hobby horse and doll, page 50).

Photographers

Most of the photographs in this book, including left and center photos on back cover, are by Darrow M. Watt. The following are exceptions—Edward Bigelow: 69 top. Glenn M. Christiansen: back cover right, 24, 25 lower right, 27, 59. Robert Cox: 84 top. Gerald R. Fredrick: 80 top. Ken Hively: 56 bottom. John F. Marriott: 67. Ells Marugg: 36. Norman A. Plate: 13 bottom, 35 lower right, 38 upper right, 45 top and center, 80 bottom. Bill Ross: 52 top. Michael Tilden: 84 bottom. Peter O. Whiteley: 61, 81.